Pearson's Canal Comp...

Severn & Avon

Published by Wayzgoose
of Tatenhill Common
Staffordshire DE13 9RS
www.jmpearson.co.uk
enquiries@jmpearson.co.uk

WAYZGOOSE

Seventh edition 2011
Updated 2014 & 2016
ISBN 978 0 9562777 5 6

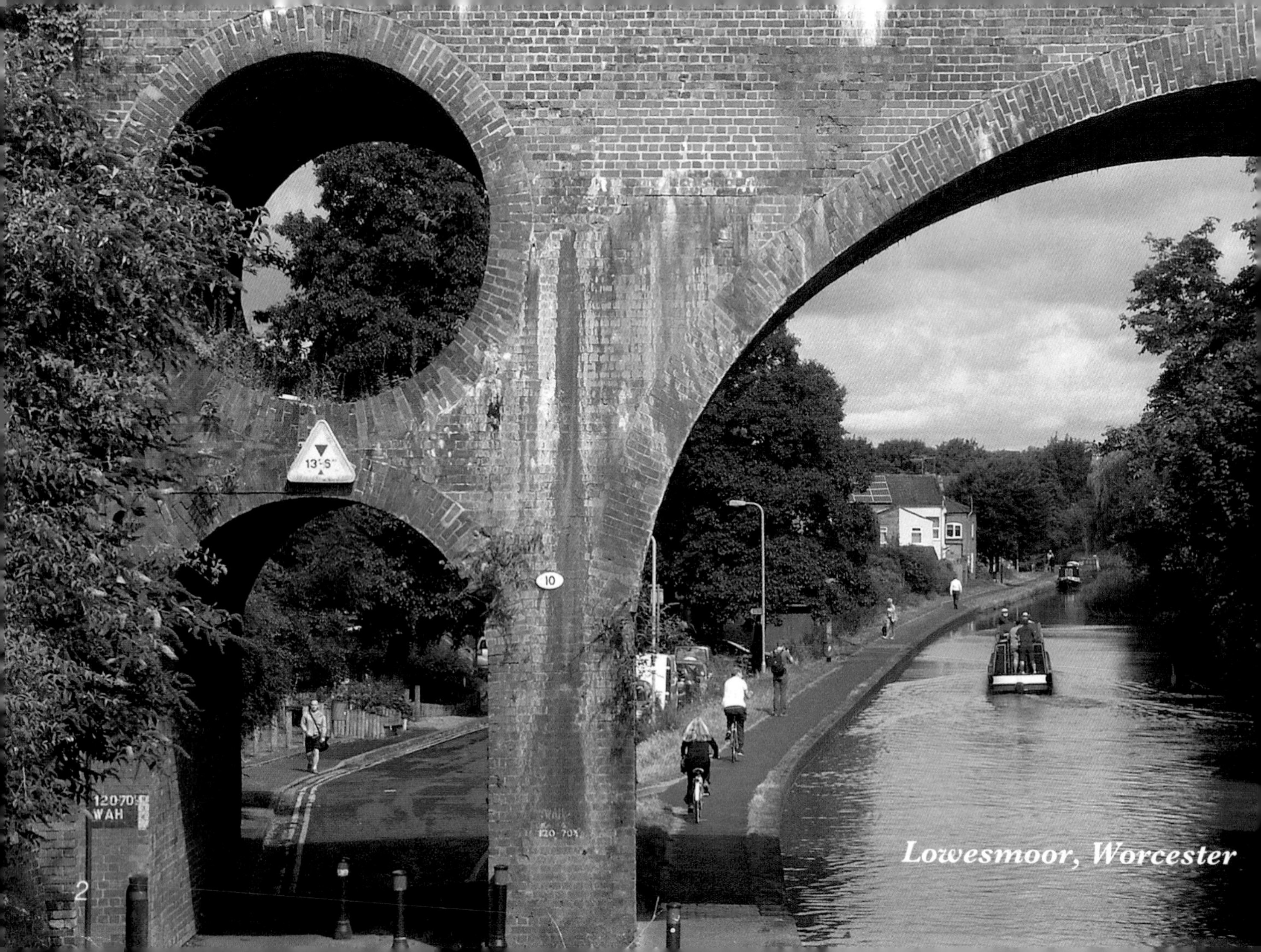

Lowesmoor, Worcester

Lock-wheeling

SCENES from a Second Reprint, Act 1: The first train of the morning had landed me in Worcester just as it was rubbing the sleep from its eyes. The last morning in March had dawned sunny, though the river was 'in the red', so to speak, coursing through the arches of the bridge at around eight knots, by my judgement. People were walking to work along the towpath. Is there a more conducive way to go? A young woman wished me a sociable 'good morning'. One of the consolations of incipient age is that girls can acknowledge you without worrying about encouraging un-sought-after advances. The cathedral was backlit by the rising sun. A plume of smoke rose from one of the adjoining properties. But whether they had chosen a new Bishop, or were just cooking the bacon for breakfast was open to conjecture. I went down as far as Diglis Locks, serene as a mill pond. Then strolled up through the basins to the Worcester & Birmingham Canal, remembering a tour of the Royal Worcester porcelain works before it was turned into a block of flats. I'd been chaperoning the South African wife of the South African CEO of the South African animal feed supplements firm I inexplicably worked for, an assignment deemed more within my powers than contributing meaningfully to the annual sales conference at the Raven Hotel in Droitwich. There must be some deep-seated psychological explanation for the fact that the more I've worked for myself, the more enjoyable factory tours have become. Back then it was a challenge to conceal my lack of enthusiasm from my august companion, and the most vivid memory of the tour was the presence in our party of a girl whose face consisted almost entirely - though far from unappealingly - of freckles.

Fondly slipping the memory back into the water, I proceeded along the towpath, savouring the W&B's languid progress through the city's urban backwaters, sharing its well-surfaced secret with postmen taking short-cuts between fish-boned streets of terraced houses. Turning into Lowesmoor, I called at the premises of ABC to check that their entry in the guide remained accurate. Reception was modelled on the *Marie Celeste* (as boatyard receptions often are), so I hung around, going through my increasingly less discreet sequence of attention-seeking devices. I was just about to whistle the chorus from *The Black Hills of Dakota* (which seldom fails to illicit an immediate response) when a business-like lady with a winning smile followed me in from outside.

"Hello," she said, "Have you been waiting long?"

"Only an hour or two," I responded; adding quickly, as her face expressed horror, that my sense of humour has a Houdini-like habit of escaping from its chains from time to time. Explaining the purpose of my visit, she disappeared in search of a colleague more versed in the minutiae of visitor mooring arrangements, returning apologetically just as I was about to grow restless again; which close friends, family and regular Canal Companion users will tell you doesn't take long.

Worcester always enraptures me, its Elgarian overtones, its ability to change face from a country town into a cathedral city at the turn of a corner. Tourist Information Centres are an endangered species, but Worcester's soldiers on in its handsome Guildhall setting, providing an exemplary service. I was thrilled to see that they stocked this very book and complimented them on their good taste and general perspicacity.

"Oh, I love these guides," exclaimed one of three ladies busying themselves behind the counter. "My husband prefers the other ones, but these are my favourite."

Expressing mild surprise that their marriage remained intact, I listened contentedly as she enumerated the Canal Companions' merits, eventually having to interrupt, firmly but politely as my head began to swell uncomfortably within the headband of my extra large Trilby. I left with her manifold endorsements ringing in my ears, musing how Worcester might justifyably add 'wonderful womenfolk' to its long list of charms.

Blossom Time, Binton Bridges

River Avon

Robin Smithett

Bidford-on-Avon

1 AVON NAVIGATION Tewkesbury 4mls/1lk/1hr

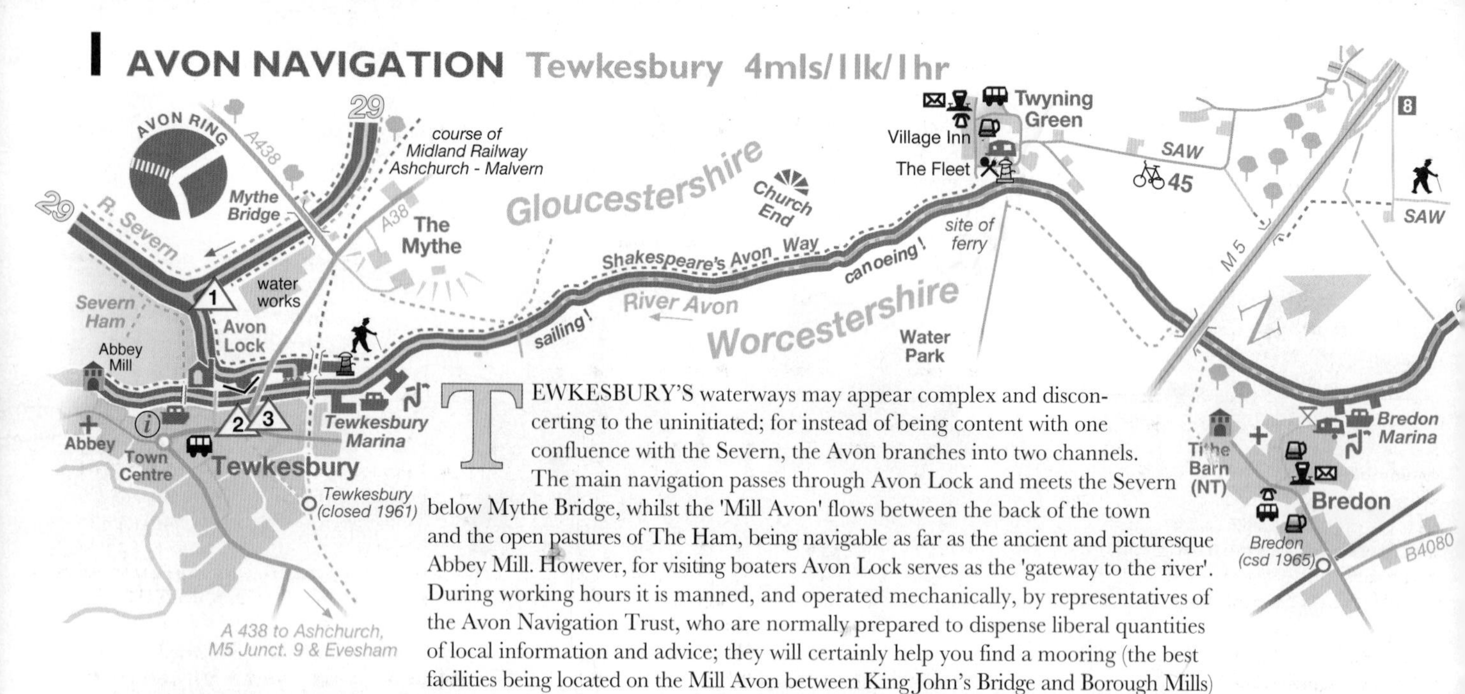

TEWKESBURY'S waterways may appear complex and disconcerting to the uninitiated; for instead of being content with one confluence with the Severn, the Avon branches into two channels. The main navigation passes through Avon Lock and meets the Severn below Mythe Bridge, whilst the 'Mill Avon' flows between the back of the town and the open pastures of The Ham, being navigable as far as the ancient and picturesque Abbey Mill. However, for visiting boaters Avon Lock serves as the 'gateway to the river'. During working hours it is manned, and operated mechanically, by representatives of the Avon Navigation Trust, who are normally prepared to dispense liberal quantities of local information and advice; they will certainly help you find a mooring (the best facilities being located on the Mill Avon between King John's Bridge and Borough Mills) and may even try and sell you something from their range of souvenirs. ANT deserve support, for without them there would be *no* navigable Avon.

Tewkesbury's waterfront is a delight. So many scenes catch the eye: the ancient arches of King John's Bridge; the quiet backwaters of the mill stream reflecting half-timbered houses and the town's towering abbey. Solely the abandoned Borough Mills introduce a sense of melancholy. Long term Canal Companion users will recall when Healings barges, *Tirley and Chaceley*, would arrive here gunwale-deep with grain transhipped at Avonmouth. A nearby bench commemorates William John (or 'Jack') Hitchman, one of Healings former skippers.

⚠ Advice for Boaters

1. Entering or leaving the Avon from or for the Severn it is important to avoid the sandbar. Give this a wide berth by keeping over towards the southern bank as you turn into the Avon, and by making sure that Mythe Bridge is in view before turning upstream into the Severn.
2. Travelling downstream you may have to wait until Avon Lock is free for your use. Try to avoid being taken past the lock entrance by the current.
3. Use the largest arch only at King John's Bridge, and proceed carefully for visibility of oncoming craft is restricted.
4. See page 94 for details of ANT's excellent *River Watch* facility.

Leaving Tewkesbury - however reluctantly - in your wake, you soon find yourself lost in a timeless landscape of lush watermeadows. The M5 motorway intrudes briefly, and noisily, into the river's secret world, before disappearing as rapidly as it arrived. And how delightfully intimate and cosy the Avon seems if you have come off the mighty Severn. How elevated your view of things, now that there are no high banks to hide the outside world. The pretty riverside villages of Twyning and Bredon - the latter well nigh impossible to visit by boat - are in different counties because this reach of the Avon forms the boundary between Gloucestershire and Worcestershire.

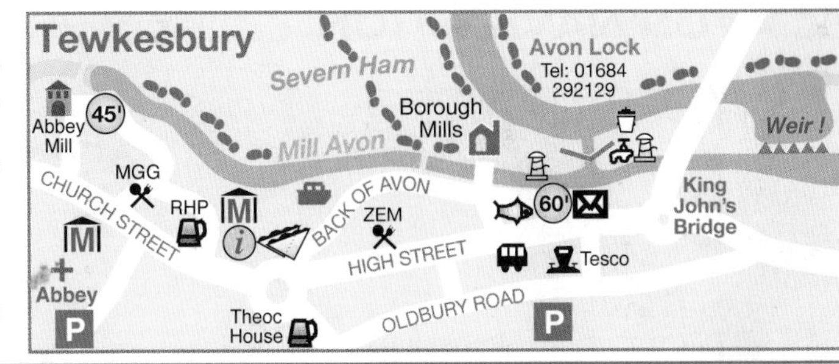

Tewkesbury

Map 1

The radiant abbey of St Mary's looms maternally over the tumbling roofs of tight-knit streets, alleyways and courtyards which lead, at dizzy intervals, to tantalizing glimpses of boats moored on the Mill Avon: when the bells ring out for evensong it is easy to imagine that the centuries have rolled back to more god-fearing times. Tewkesbury was the fictional 'Elmbury' of John Moore's *Brensham Trilogy*, glorious post-war portraits of a Gloucestershire market town and its hinterland.

Eating & Drinking

KINGFISHER - Quay Street. Tel: 01684 293220. Splendid fish & chip shop/cafe. GL20 5BE

MY GREAT GRANDFATHERS - Church Street. Tel: 01684 292687. Excellent restaurant. GL20 5RX

ROYAL HOP POLE - Church Street. Tel: 01684 274039/278670. Well-loved Tewkesbury watering hole, which Dickens had Mr Pickwick visit. GL20 5RS

THEOC HOUSE - Barton Street. Tel: 01684 296562. *Good Beer Guide* listed blend of cafe/pub. GL20 5PY

ZITTO E MANGIA - High Street. Tel: 01684 297017. Delightful Italian restaurant. GL20 5AT

Shopping

A lovely town to shop in, but do beware the narrow pavements and traffic which appears reluctant to take prisoners. 1471 (named after the battle, you know) is an admirable delicatessen by The Cross, a great place to head for when making up picnics. Food for the brain can be sourced at three bookshops: Alison's on High Street is an excellent example of how an independent bookseller (new) can thrive, and they have a nice line in classical music as well. Almost next door is Cornell Books (alongside Barclays Bank) who are especially strong on s/h topography and old OS mapping - encourage the charming owner to reminisce about 'Spanky Dyson' - whilst also on High Street is Bookworms (s/h). But if it's more mundane merchandise that you're seeking, there are Tesco and Co-op supermarkets. Market days are Wednesday and Saturday, and there's a Farmers Market on the second Saturday in the month.

Things to Do

TOURIST INFORMATION & HERITAGE CENTRE - Church Street. Tel: 01684 855040. Local history displays housed in former hat shop. Particularly good section devoted to the town's two rivers. GL20 5AB

JOHN MOORE COUNTRYSIDE MUSEUM - Church Street. Tel: 01684 297174. Small admission charge. Open Tue-Sat Apr-Oct plus Bank Holidays and Saturdays and school holidays in winter. Timber-framed 15th century town house devoted to interpretations of natural history and the literary output of John Moore, a number of whose books are on sale. Admission fee also provides access to neighbouring Merchant's House and cottage garden. GL20 5SN

TEWKESBURY ABBEY - Church Street. Tel: 01684 850959. Open daily. The visitor's centre features displays and exhibitions, as well as a refectory overlooking the abbey grounds. Ascents of the tower (212 steps) may be booked in advance. GL20 5RZ

Connections

BUSES - Service 41/2 links Tewkesbury with Cheltenham at frequent intervals and additionally provides a link to/from Ashchurch railway station. Service 351operates Mon-Sat to/from Gloucester via Ashleworth, whilst service 71 operates a more direct hourly Mon-Sat link to/from Gloucester. 540 runs to/from Evesham via Bredon. Tel: 0871 200 2233.

TRAINS - Ashchurch (for Tewkesbury) station lies two miles east. Tel: 03457 484950. Bus connections.

TAXIS - Avonside. Tel: 01684 293916.

Twyning Green

New visitor moorings provide welcome access to two good pubs and a post office store.

2 AVON NAVIGATION Eckington & Comberton 6mls/2lks/2hrs

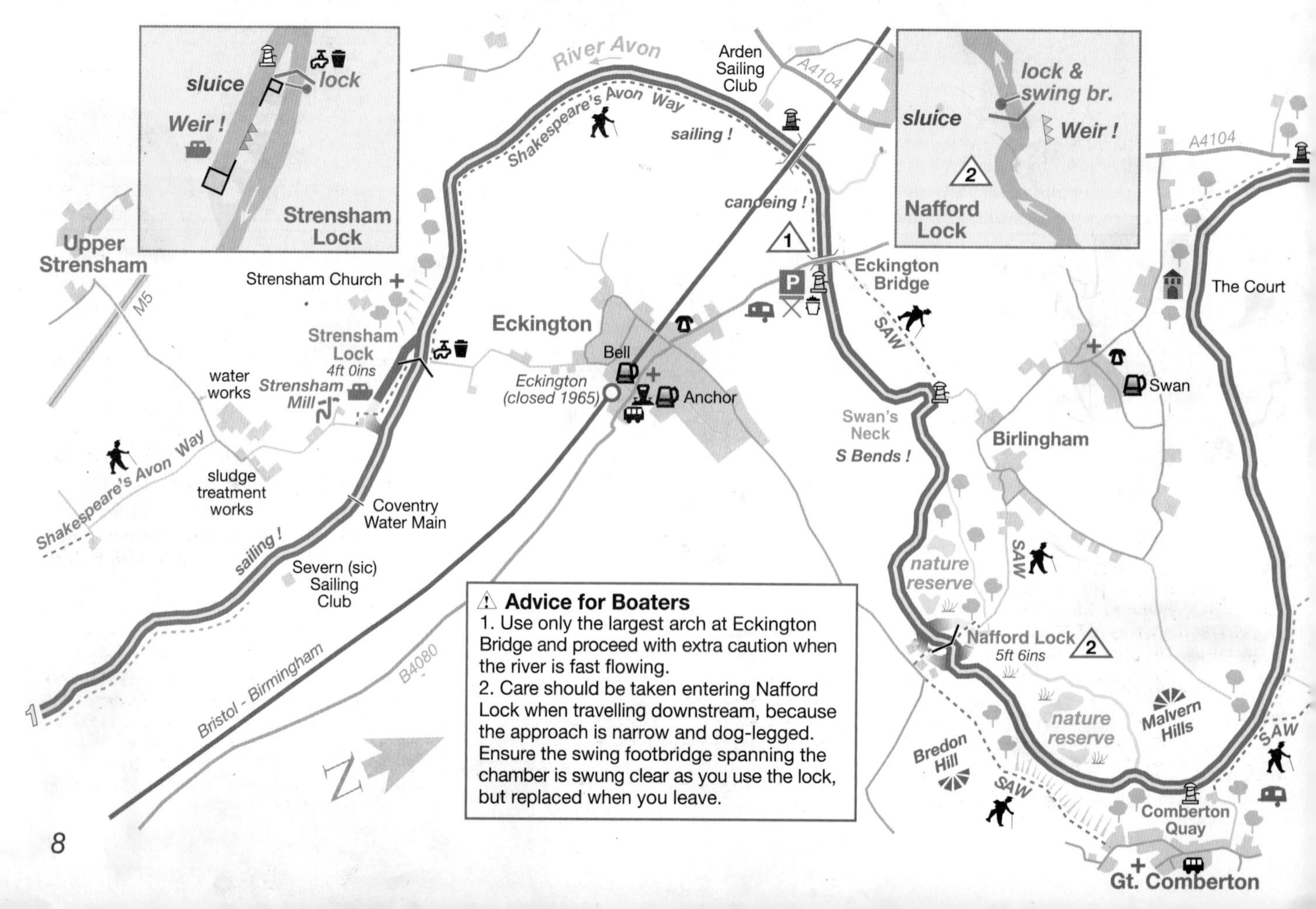

⚠ **Advice for Boaters**

1. Use only the largest arch at Eckington Bridge and proceed with extra caution when the river is fast flowing.
2. Care should be taken entering Nafford Lock when travelling downstream, because the approach is narrow and dog-legged. Ensure the swing footbridge spanning the chamber is swung clear as you use the lock, but replaced when you leave.

THE Avon seems infatuated by Bredon Hill, hardly letting it out of its sight, fascinated by the summit's constantly changing shape. Half wooded, half bare, like mottled baize, it forms an island between the Cotswold Edge and the distant serrated outline of the Malvern Hills. Because its peak falls short of a thousand feet, the squire of Kemerton Court (on the southern flank of the hill) erected a folly on its top so that he could stand that high above sea level. Another distinctive feature of Bredon is its Iron Age fort.

This Avon is second only to the Thames in the amount of writing it has inspired, and this stretch is particularly rich in literary associations. Every guidebook quotes A. E. Housman's poem *In Summertime on Bredon* (an odd geographical aberration for a set of poems entitled *A Shropshire Lad*), but a better poem was written by Sir Arthur Quiller-Couch about Eckington Bridge. 'Q' had canoed the river as a young man in 1890, and had been inspired to compose a magnificent ode to the bridge which speaks of 'eloquent grooves worn into the sandstone by labouring bargemen'. Quiller-Couch also employed the river in his adventurous tale *True Tilda*, painting an especially evocative scene of the bustling barges and steam tugs at Tewkesbury. Following his own journey down the river in 1910, Temple Thurston used Nafford Mill (destroyed by fire in 1909) as the setting for his Richard Furlong trilogy, now long-forgotten and out of print, but still wonderful reading if you can find them (as it is reasonably easy to do) second-hand. Other literary associations include the local writer John Moore who called it 'Brensham Hill' and the children's author Ursula Moray Williams who lived the latter part of her life at Beckford on the south-west side of the hill. It is not difficult to see why such writers were moved to capture the spirit of this quintessentially English landscape. It would be one of life's missed opportunities, were you not to moor, at Comberton Quay or Eckington Bridge, make an ascent of Bredon Hill, and see for yourself Housman's 'coloured counties' and *your* river, meandering through this peerless panorama like a wandering minstrel.

Strensham Lock was formerly overlooked by two mills. Being separated from the M5 by a church-topped hill (St John the Baptist, with its curiously cream-washed tower, is in the capable hands of the Churches Conservation Trust), it could be a million miles from the motorway service area that shares its name. Either side of the lock the river roams pensively past shallow banks of reeds and lily-pads, rutted by cattle and sheep intent on quenching their thirst. Downstream of Eckington's marvellously medieval bridge, in a reach plied by sailing craft from the Arden club, the busy Bristol-Derby railway crosses the river by way of a not ungraceful iron span resting on stone piers. Herbert Spencer, the influential Victorian philosopher and plausible inventor of the 'slip' coach, was instrumental in its design during a youthful sojourn in the engineering offices of the Birmingham & Gloucester Railway.

Eckington — Map 2

Worcestershire village idyllically located on the pleated hem of Bredon Hill but prone to flooding when the Avon bursts its banks. The church is usually open and inside is a monument to John Hanford of Woollas (5965) Hall, his wife and their *thirteen* children. Picnic site and circular walk by Eckington Bridge.

Eating & Drinking

THE BELL - Church Street. Tel: 01386 750033. Refurbished country pub. Accommodation. WR10 3AN

THE ANCHOR - Cotheridge Lane. Tel: 01386 750356. Cosy 17th century village pub offering B&B. Bar & restaurant food. Piddle ales and guests. WR10 3BA

Shopping

Excellent village stores.

Connections

BUSES - service 382 operates daily to/from Pershore and Worcester. Tel: 0871 200 2233.

Birlingham — Map 2

Isolated village accessible both to walkers on Shakespeare's Avon Way and boaters who can moor most romantically at the Swan's Neck

Eating & Drinking

SWAN INN - Church Street. Tel: 01386 750485. Half a millennium old, this welcoming thatched and half-timbered, *Good Beer Guide* listed country inn is difficult to pass unvisited. Home cooked meals, Wye Valley Bitter and guest ales. WR10 3AQ

Great Comberton — Map 2

Shopless and publess but possessed of a community library intriguingly housed in a telephone kiosk. The rules are simple and might usefully be adopted by far grander libraries: you take back what you borrow or provide a suitable replacement. The parish church of St Michael is honey coloured, surrounded by yews, and inviting, but not, apparently, as trusting as the telephone kiosk.

3 AVON NAVIGATION Pershore 6mls/2lks/2hrs

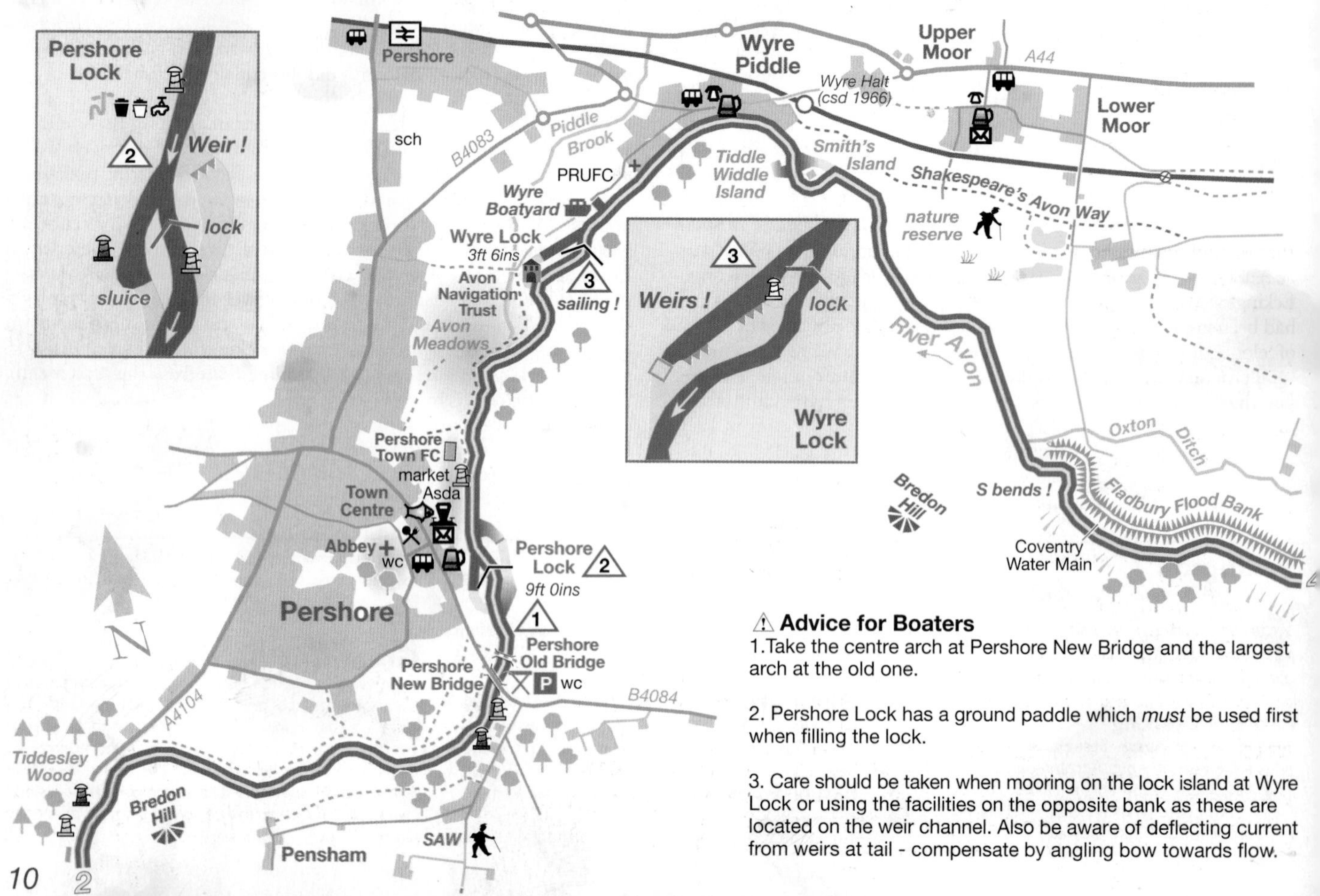

⚠ Advice for Boaters

1. Take the centre arch at Pershore New Bridge and the largest arch at the old one.

2. Pershore Lock has a ground paddle which *must* be used first when filling the lock.

3. Care should be taken when mooring on the lock island at Wyre Lock or using the facilities on the opposite bank as these are located on the weir channel. Also be aware of deflecting current from weirs at tail - compensate by angling bow towards flow.

ENTRENCHED in the Vale of Evesham, the Avon makes its stately way past Tiddesley Wood, where the famous Pershore 'Egg' plum was discovered growing wild in 1833. Pollarded willows and swaying poplars betray the river's course as it meanders towards the sturdy tower of Pershore Abbey. The original bridge at Pershore dates from the 14th century and contrives to look even older. Military men have always had a love/hate relationship with bridges, and the Cavaliers tried to demolish this one as they escaped from the Battle of Worcester in 1651. Thankfully it stood its ground. Seemingly nothing could mar the charm of its setting or its own inherent beauty. Nothing, that is, until the motor car came along, demanding construction of a straighter, flatter span. Built in 1928, it was hailed as the first concrete bridge in Worcestershire, though sadly not the last. Pershore Mill was destroyed by fire in 1971, the fate of so many mills. It had been the last mill on the Avon in commercial use, and was also the river's last source of traffic. A little barge, with the biblical name of *Pisgah*, traded to and from the mill until the end.

Wyre Lock is diamond shaped: many of the original Avon locks were of unusual configuration to reduce erosion of the chambers by the force of water from the sluices. The Avon Navigation Trust have offices and workshops located in the old mill at Wyre. Desirable residences create an enviable riverside environment for the villagers of Wyre Piddle, but upstream the river soon loses itself amongst the fruit fields and orchards of this fertile valley. Herons and kingfishers abound. Shakespeare's Avon Way loses touch with the river again. Time hangs motionlessly over the landscape like the cobwebby pendulum of an unwound grandfather clock. Fladbury flood bank dates from 1881. Four feet high, it has sluice valves built into its bank to protect the farmlands from the ravages of the river. The flood bank hasn't always been up to its task, as several high water marks in Fladbury village testify.

Pershore

Map 3

Balconies blossoming from Georgian houses lend a holiday feel, an inherent *joie de vivre* to Pershore, best known nowadays, not for pears as the name implies, but for rich, ruby red plums. Asparagus (or 'gras') is another local delicacy, widely available between March and June. The Abbey, only marginally less imposing than Tewkesbury's, was only partially demolished following the Dissolution of the Monasteries. John Betjeman wrote of the abbey bells being rung for evensong in a poem called *Pershore Station*. Boaters are afforded easy access to the town centre over playing fields and past an impressive leisure centre with swimming pool.

Eating & Drinking

BELLE HOUSE TRAITEUR - Bridge Street. Tel: 01386 555055. Stylish modern restaurant/deli. WR10 1AJ

WHISTLERS - Royal Arcade. Tel: 01386 556900 Amiable first floor bistro overlooking the sweep of Broad Street. Balcony tables. WR10 1AG

BRANDY CASK - Bridge Street. Tel: 01386 552602. Time-warp interior, gorgeous garden with hungry carp and limited customer moorings. Home-brewed beer plus guests. Wholesome budget-priced food. *Good Beer Guide* entry. WR10 1AJ

PICKLED PLUM - High Street. Tel: 01386 556645. Gastropub at the north end of High Street. WR10 1EQ

SHUNARGA - High Street. Tel: 01386 555357. Asian fusion. WR10 1DP

Shopping

Many boaters venture no further than Asda's supermarket adjacent to the riverside recreation ground, but it would be a shame to miss out on the many antique and book shops sprinkled liberally around the town. There are also a butcher, baker, two delicatessens and a launderette. Retailers tend to be in for the long haul here: Elts have been selling shoes since 1872, and Browns ironmongery since 1913. The indoor retail market operates Wednesday through Saturday.

Connections

BUSES - services 550/1 to/from Worcester and Evesham. Local bus 383 links the town centre to the railway station. Tel: 0871 200 2233.

TRAINS - Cotswold Line services by First Great Western Tel: 03457 484950.

TAXIS - Richmond Taxis. Tel: 01386 710335.

Wyre Piddle

Map 3

One of those comically named English villages which tickle the vulgar fancy, Wyre has lent its name to a beer, though that's actually brewed by Ambridge in Inkberrow. Pershore Rugby Club play at Piddle Park; cue for much ribaldry from visiting teams.

Eating & Drinking

ANCHOR INN - Tel: 01386 244590. Much refurbished after a period of closure, but still providing moorings for patrons. Pleasant decking overlooking the river and Bredon Hill. Closed Mondays. WR10 2JB

River Avon

Pershore Abbey

Robin Smithett

Evesham Lock

Eckington Bridge

Cropthorne

Robin Smithett

Fladbury Lock

ain Ferry

Royal Shakespeare Theatre

Robin Smithett

Holy Trinity

Robin Smithett

Weir Brake Lock

Robin Smithett

Luddington Lock

Robin Smithett

Bancroft Basin

Robin Smithett

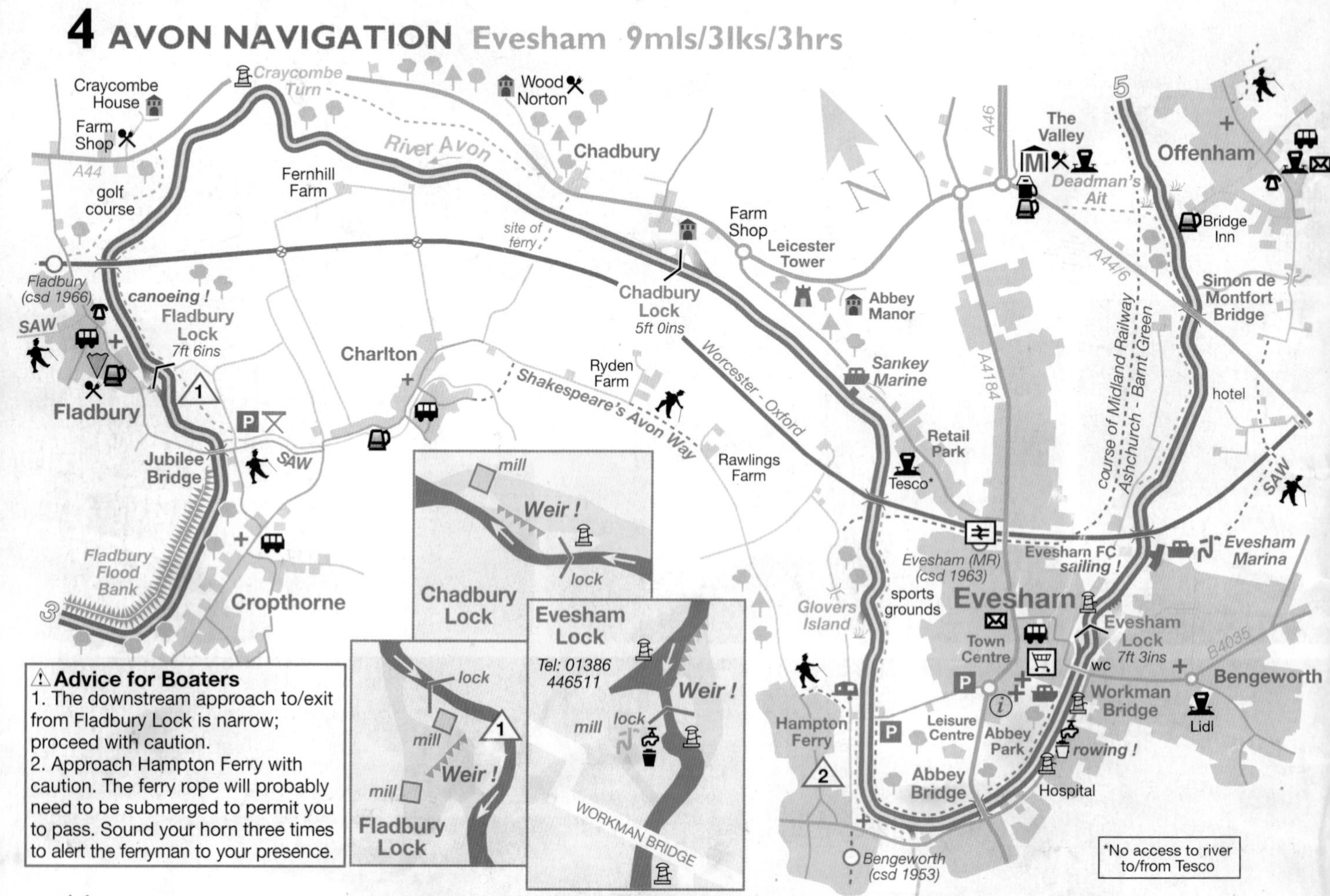
4 AVON NAVIGATION Evesham 9mls/3lks/3hrs
Craycombe House
Farm Shop
A44
golf course
Craycombe Turn
Wood Norton
River Avon
Chadbury
Fernhill Farm
site of ferry
Farm Shop
Leicester Tower
Abbey Manor
Chadbury Lock
5ft 0ins
Fladbury (csd 1966)
canoeing !
Fladbury Lock
7ft 6ins
SAW
Fladbury
Charlton
Ryden Farm
Shakespeare's Avon Way
Worcester - Oxford
Jubilee Bridge
Rawlings Farm
Fladbury Flood Bank
Cropthorne
A46
The Valley
Deadman's Ait
Offenham
Bridge Inn
A44/6
Simon de Montfort Bridge
course of Midland Railway Ashchurch - Barnt Green
Sankey Marine
A4184
Retail Park
Tesco*
hotel
Evesham (MR) (csd 1963)
Evesham FC
sailing !
Evesham Marina
Glovers Island
sports grounds
Evesham
Town Centre
Evesham Lock
7ft 3ins
wc
B4035
Bengeworth
Workman Bridge
Lidl
Leisure Centre
Abbey Park
rowing !
Hampton Ferry
Abbey Bridge
Hospital
Bengeworth (csd 1953)
*No access to river to/from Tesco
Chadbury Lock
mill
Weir !
lock
Evesham Lock
Tel: 01386 446511
Weir !
lock
mill
WORKMAN BRIDGE
Fladbury Lock
lock
mill
Weir !
mill
Advice for Boaters
1. The downstream approach to/exit from Fladbury Lock is narrow; proceed with caution.
2. Approach Hampton Ferry with caution. The ferry rope will probably need to be submerged to permit you to pass. Sound your horn three times to alert the ferryman to your presence.

EVESHAM marked the frontier between what used to be known as the Lower and Upper navigable sections of the River Avon, restored and administered by separate trusts but now under the aegis of one combined body. Following decades of disuse, the Lower Avon was re-opened to navigation in 1962, the Upper in 1974; blithe dates which do scant justice to the monies raised and volunteer labour involved in restoring the river to the state that so many people enjoy today.

Between Cropthorne and Offenham the river practically boxes the compass on its gorgeous meanderings through the vegetable-growing vale. In the 19th century the only way to cross the river at Cropthorne was to ford it. But in Queen Victoria's Jubilee year a bridge was built to span the river here, so that Fladbury lads could go courting Cropthorne lasses without necessarily getting their feet wet. One of the river's last working water-gates occupied the reach below Jubilee Bridge. These were devices for altering water levels without adversely affecting supplies to the mills. A conventional lock here would have lowered the water level to the detriment of the mill at Wyre. The water-gate provided a simple alternative. It consisted of a gate fitted with sluices set into a weir. In normal circumstances the gate would remain open until a boat passed through on its way upstream. Then the gate would be closed while the boat waited for a sufficient level of water to be built up to enable it to navigate up to Fladbury Lock. On the way back the sluices would be drawn on reaching the gate, and there a boat would wait until the levels had equalised and the gate could be opened. L. T. C. Rolt described its use in *Landscape With Machines*. He and his fiancee, Angela, had hired a cabin cruiser called *Miranda* from a boatyard at Wyre Piddle in 1938 in order to 'test the water' prior to plunging into full-time life afloat with *Cressy* as seminally related in his timeless classic *Narrow Boat*.

Fladbury

Robin Smithett

The Avon at Fladbury is the stuff of dreams. Once there were two mills, that beside the lock being known as Cropthorne Mill in deference to its position. It is linked to the outside world by a private rope ferry. The other, quite naturally, was called Fladbury Mill and in latter years a pair of Armfield 20hp turbines were installed to provide the village with electricity. Grandiosely known as the Fladbury Electric Light & Power Co., they charged ten shillings per light per annum to householders in the district.The rhyming locks at Fladbury and Chadbury deserve a poem about them. Certainly there is plenty of inspiration in the landscape as the river winds past the orcharded flanks of Craycombe and Wood Norton. Craycombe House - guarded by a tall cedar - was built for George Perrott, an 18th century owner of the navigation. The novelist Francis Brett Young lived in it during the Thirties. Wood Norton Hall was ostentatiously erected in 1897 for the Duke of Orleans, pretender to the French throne. During the Second World War it became a BBC centre for radio monitoring of foreign stations, and quite possibly Hitler's death was first learned of here. In response to the Cold War a deep nuclear bunker was added: light entertainment for the survivors, perhaps? Chadbury Lock, formerly diamond-shaped, was the first to be rebuilt by the Lower Avon Navigation Trust in 1953. Much of the work was done by the Royal Engineers, a pioneering use of military resources on a civilian project.

continued overleaf:

continued from page 15:

Above the treetops bordering the next reach stands the Leicester Tower, built in 1840 as a memorial to Simon de Montfort, the Earl of Leicester, who came a cropper at the Battle of Evesham in 1265. The monks of Evesham Abbey planted vineyards on these south-facing slopes in the Middle Ages. Round the corner two railway bridges spanned the river. One remains, carrying the highly scenic Cotswolds & Malverns line. The other - a client of the ferroequinological firm of undertakers, Beeching & Marples - carried the Midland Railway route from Redditch to Ashchurch near Tewkesbury. If it had remained open north of Evesham at least, it might have been more than a little useful as a commuter link with Birmingham today, a mere sixteen miles of railway permanently lost through dubiously reached and short-sighted, accountancy-led thinking. The abandoned abutments of the vanished bridge retain a latent dignity as exemplified by their ochre-coloured corner stones.

Hampton Ferry

Glass houses, glinting in the sunlight, emphasise Evesham's reputation as a fruit growing centre, as the river skirts its western suburbs and you pass the flourishing ferry at Hampton. This is one of only two public ferries still in existence on the Avon. It provides a popular short cut for the inhabitants of a static caravan site to reach Evesham's shops. There is an aesthetic pleasure in its to-ing and fro-ing which makes you sad that not more of the river's ferries have survived. Local authorities, one feels, might have done more to preserve such operations, if only to maintain the integrity of public rights of way. Letting slip to the amiable ferryman that we'd walked the twenty miles from Tewkesbury that day, he replied: "I thought nothing of thirty-five with a tent on my back in my day"!

Abbey Bridge was renewed - to the tune of £8 million - in 2014. Its airy, modern, bowspring design contrasts with that of Workman Bridge, named after one of the town's Victorian mayors, which spans the river in the centre of Evesham. Recreation grounds, bordered by an avenue of limes, create a gracious riverside environment. On hot days, with Evesham *en fete*, you might be reminded of Seurat's pointillistic masterpiece of the *La Grande Jatte.* Rowing sculls, 'fours' and 'eights', skiffs and motor boats, trip boats et al add to the general sense of busyness here throughout the summer months, and there will be occasions when the passing boater finds it difficult to either manoeuvre or moor. Such activities hark back to an Edwardian heyday when steamers regularly plied the river between Evesham and Tewkesbury.

Evesham Lock is the highest upstream on the Lower Avon. A triangular-shaped lock-keeper's house spans the original, long since disused chamber. A self-operated pump-out facility has been introduced here. Adjoining mills have been converted into apartments.

Between Evesham and Offenham the river is left pretty much to its own devices. The railway and the by-pass cross the Avon but leave little impression on it. Beyond the watermeadows, and the likelihood of floods, the countryside is thick with regimented fruit trees and the ubiquitous green houses in which Evesham's reputation as a centre for the cultivation of tomato plants is forged.

Deadman's Ait was the scene of heavy fighting during the Battle of Evesham. Many Welshmen were slaughtered in the vicinity, and large quantities of human remains were unearthed during the eighteenth century. The peace we associate with the English landscape had to be fought for. Offenham is known throughout the district for its annual 'wake', a week of fun and frivolity at the beginning of June. Notwithstanding signposts in the village, the ferry, apparently, ceased operating in the early Sixties, though you have to go back a couple of centuries earlier to find the bridge which gave the pub its name.

Fladbury Map 4

Alas and alack, the absence for many years of suitable moorings has rendered the pretty village of Fladbury effectively beyond the reach of boaters. Slim wonder it is no longer capable of sustaining a general store. Temple Thurston would feel betrayed and Mrs Izod aghast that the ferry no longer operates for the benefit of the public and radish pickers. The railway station is another victim of the passage of time. Once its goods yard 'reeked with fruit', local plums went all the way to a jam factory in Lancashire, and savoy cabbages spilled on to the rails they were stacked so high.

Eating & Drinking

ANCHOR INN - village green. Tel: 01386 860391. Welcoming village local offering B&B. WR10 2PY.
CHEQUERS INN - Tel: 01386 861854. Country pub with rooms and 'high end' cooking. WR10 2PZ
CRAYCOMBE CAFE - Craycombe Farm (A44). Tel: 01386 860732. Tea rooms and deli accessible from Craycombe Turn moorings but take care of traffic. Antiques/collectibles outlet next door. WR10 2QS

Shopping

Fladbury Pies & Sausages make the mouth water, and their little emporium opposite the church is open Tue-Sat, EC Thur & Sat. Tel: 01386 860228.

Connections

BUSES - infrequent peak-hour services to/from Pershore and Worcester in one direction and Evesham in the other. Tel: 0871 200 2233.

Evesham Map 4

Iron Curtain accents proliferate in Evesham, cynosure of its fruity vale. The by-pass and pedestrianisation between them seem to have created a semblance of calm that has been absent since the invention of the motor car. Highlights include the Bell Tower, all that's left of an abbey demolished following the Dissolution. Compare its fate with Pershore, losing only its nave and Tewkesbury, surviving virtually intact. Time your visit to hear the tower's carillon - playing *Linden Lea* when we last paused, rapt, to listen. Standing alongside is St Lawrence's, cared for by those paragons, the Churches Conservation Trust. Some of its stained glass is the work of Frederick Preedy, born in Offenham in 1820, and a prolific designer of church architecture and glass throughout the Vale of Evesham and beyond. Indeed examples of his windows can be found in the cathedrals of Worcester, Gloucester, Ely and Lincoln. On the Bengeworth side of the river, The Regal is a fine example of Art Deco cinema architecture and includes a good cafe.

Eating & Drinking

BREW BEAR - High Street. Tel: 01386 761213. Excellent coffee shop up beyond post office. WR11 4DA
ROYAL OAK - Vine Street. Tel: 01386 442465. Half-timbered town centre pub which boasts award-winning chef. Hogs Back & Purity ales. WR11 4RE
WORD OF MOUTH - Vine Street. Tel: 01386 422259. 'Local, lovely & independent' is the strap line for this charming and allergy-aware cafe located between the Bell Tower and the TIC. WR11 4RL

Shopping

Bridge Street and High Street are the principal shopping thoroughfares, along with the River Side indoor shopping centre, the latter being the site for many of the well known chain stores. But don't ignore Bengeworth, east of the river, which has a bike shop, launderette, pharmacy, a plethora of East European food stores, heaps of takeaways, and a Lidl. Regrettably, the large Tesco which overlooks the river on the western edge of town is inaccessible therefrom.

Things to Do

TOURIST INFORMATION - The Almonry, Abbey Gate. Tel: 01386 446944. WR11 4BG
ALMONRY HERITAGE CENTRE - Abbey Gate. Tel: 01386 446944. Open Mon-Sat 10am-5pm and Suns (Mar-Oct) 2-5pm. Small admission charge. The former home of the Abbey Almoner today houses a heritage centre detailing the history of the town. WR11 4BG
THE VALLEY - Twyford. Tel: 01386 298026. Countrified retail complex on the northern outskirts of town. Farm shop, garden centre, cafe/restaurant etc. Again, no direct access from river, unfortunately! WR11 4TP
EVESHAM VALE LIGHT RAILWAY - an integral attaction to the above, this mile long, 15 inch gauge railway runs through orchards and regularly features some classic motive power including two Atlantics: *John* built for the Rhyl Miniature Railway in 1921 and Bassett-Lowke's *Count Louis* of 1924. Tel: 01386 422282.
HANDSAM BOAT CO - skiffs, motorboats and river trips - Tel: 0786 089 5416. WR11 4ST

Connections

BUSES - First Midland Red service X50 links Evesham with Pershore and Worcester hourly Mon-Sat. Service 540, operated by Astons of Kempsey, runs hourly Mon-Sat to/from Tewkesbury offering a magical mystery tour of Bredon Hill in the process. For Stratford via Bidford catch Johnsons service X18. Tel: 0871 200 2233.
TRAINS - Great Western Railway Cotswold & Malvern Line services to/from Worcester via Pershore and London Paddington via Oxford. Tel: 03457 484950.
TAXIS - BR Taxis. Tel: 01386 830066.

Offenham Map 4

Market gardening village with maypole.

Eating & Drinking

BRIDGE INN - riverside with customer moorings. Tel: 01386 446565. Charmingly located with nice waterside garden. House ale brewed by Wye Valley, bar & bistro food. Open from 11am daily. WR11 8QZ

5 AVON NAVIGATION Harvington 5mls/3lks/2hrs

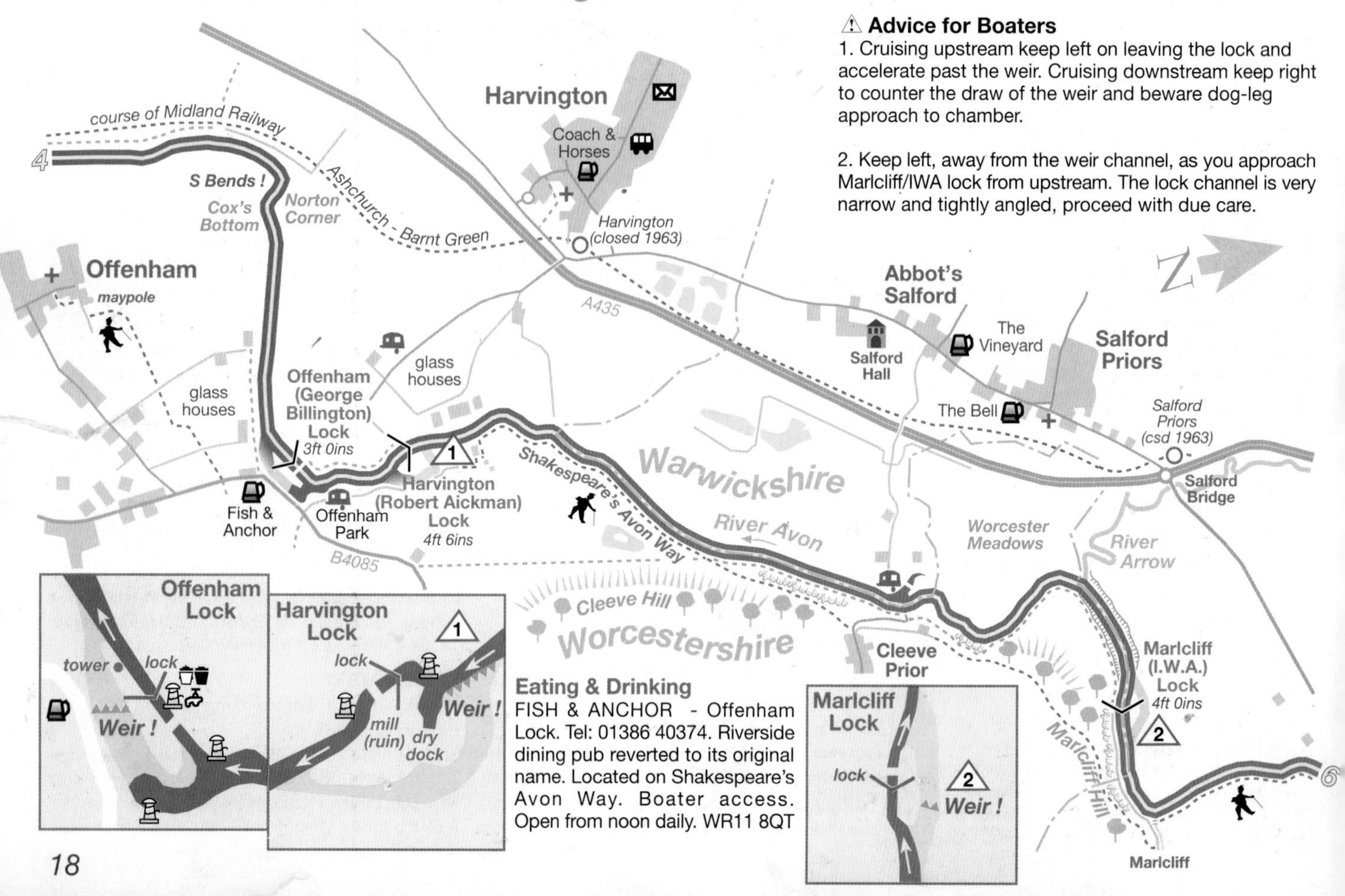

⚠ Advice for Boaters

1. Cruising upstream keep left on leaving the lock and accelerate past the weir. Cruising downstream keep right to counter the draw of the weir and beware dog-leg approach to chamber.

2. Keep left, away from the weir channel, as you approach Marlcliff/IWA lock from upstream. The lock channel is very narrow and tightly angled, proceed with due care.

Eating & Drinking

FISH & ANCHOR - Offenham Lock. Tel: 01386 40374. Riverside dining pub reverted to its original name. Located on Shakespeare's Avon Way. Boater access. Open from noon daily. WR11 8QT

DRIFTING through time and space, the Avon wends its secluded way between Evesham and Bidford. Hitherto, boaters have more or less enjoyed exclusive access to these reaches of the river, but with the development of *Shakespeare's Avon Way* ramblers have acquired a more robust route; well signposted, reasonably well maintained, and stretching 88 miles from the Avon's source at Naseby in Northamptonshire to Tewkesbury.

Substantially different in character to the lower river, the Upper Avon has a wilder feel to it, akin perhaps to the uppermost reaches of the River Thames between Oxford and Lechlade. It was appropriate, therefore, that second-hand paddle gear from Thames locks was used in the restoration of the Upper Avon. And what a mammoth undertaking it was, costing more than six times as much as the Lower Avon restoration project.

All the Upper Avon locks are dual-named after individuals or groups associated with the restoration of the river. The work at Offenham/George Billington Lock was completed in just six weeks so that its donor, who was terminally ill in his thirties, might observe the effect of his benefaction before he died. Harvington/Robert Aickman Lock commemorates one of the most influential figures of the post war inland waterways renaissance. Aickman founded the Inland Waterways Association in 1946 and crusaded for the waterways cause for a further twenty years. Returning navigation to the Avon was dear to his heart, and he was on the council of both Trusts. A memorial plaque, set in an attractive sweep of brickwork, graces the lockside, paying homage to his achievements and determination.

More practically, the boater is thankful for the provision of free overnight moorings on most Upper Avon lock cuts, many located in blissfully remote rural surroundings. From Offenham Lock it's a pleasant mile's walk along Anchor Lane to Harvington with its distinctive copper-spired church. The late David Hutchings, who masterminded resoration of the Upper Avon, lived here in a house he'd built out of an old railway bridge. The moorings at Harvington Lock provide access to the village as well, whilst you can also view the ruins of an old water mill which hasn't worked in a century.

Sir Arthur Quiller-Couch wrote of 'clouds of sweet-smelling flour' issuing from the doorway of Cleeve Mill, but virtually all trace of the lock, weir and mill at Cleeve has vanished. Up until the Second World War this was a popular venue for picnics. Below the weir the Avon was shallow enough to be forded by hay carts at harvest time. A correspondent from Canada wrote to tell us that his great uncle once lived in the mill, commuting from Salford Priors station to Birmingham, where he was the conductor of the symphony orchestra and on personal terms with Tchaikovsky:what interesting people the *Canal Companion* users are!

Downstream of the Marlcliff/I.W.A. Lock, the River Arrow has its confluence with the Avon. Consideration was given to making this navigable in the 17th century, but nothing materialised. The Arrow rises on the Lickey Hills and passes through the lower reservoir at Bittell beside the Worcester & Birmingham Canal, so you may well see it again. Likewise its tributary, the Alne, which follows the Stratford Canal for a while in the vicinity of Preston Bagot.

Marlcliffe is aptly named, for the Trust had considerable problems during the construction of the lock, due to the unyielding quality of the substrata. ANT's handbook describes many of the difficulties overcome during the restoration in a matter of fact way, a modesty which fails to disguise the vast amount of work they undertook - and continue to undertake - on our behalf.

6 AVON NAVIGATION Bidford & Welford 6mls/3lks/2.5hrs

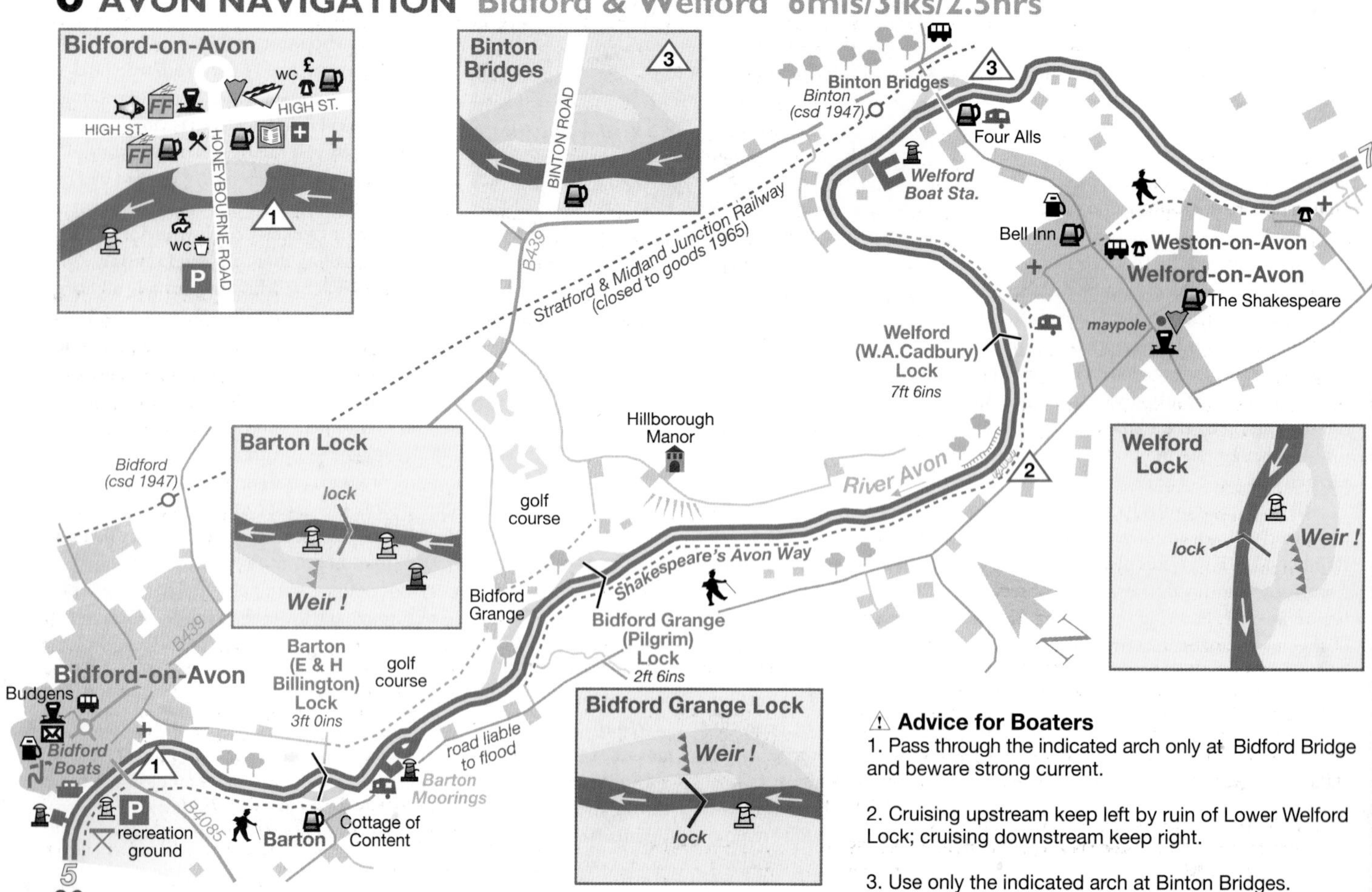

⚠ **Advice for Boaters**

1. Pass through the indicated arch only at Bidford Bridge and beware strong current.

2. Cruising upstream keep left by ruin of Lower Welford Lock; cruising downstream keep right.

3. Use only the indicated arch at Binton Bridges.

NARROW and winding - rather after the fashion of life itself - the Upper Avon is at its loveliest between Bidford and Weston. Like dividends from a sagaciously garnered investment portfolio, the locks - not always situated in exact accordance with those on the original navigation - come at satisfying intervals, but the rest of the time you have every justification for just sitting back and watching the peaceful landscape slip uneventfully astern, grateful that there were believers enough to restore navigability to the river. Reflect that the attitudes of landowners, local and water authorities influenced the final shape of restoration. Sometimes such individuals and bodies were extraordinarily helpful, whilst others seemed determined to stop the scheme in its tracks. Inexplicably, as Robert Aickman put it, the restorers were not always seen to be on the side of the angels.

Bidford positively bristles with boats, coming in to moor with varying degrees of proficiency, or threading their way gingerly through the eye of a needle navigation arch of the 15th Century bridge. Old cronies gossip on the cutwaters, enjoying a private joke or two at the expense of the less adept boaters, or eyeing with obvious relish the amount of flesh exposed by female boaters on hot days.

The Romans elected to cross the Avon at Bidford. Their Ryknild Street forded the river here on its way to the town of Alcester. Later the road was known as Buckle Street, and it was the monks of Alcester who erected the present bridge which dates from 1482. None of its seven arches are alike in size or shape, and it still looks so medieval that the regular passage across the narrow span of lorries and double-decker buses appears ridiculously anachronistic. The official moorings at Bidford provide sufficient space for only three or four narrowboats alongside the Recreation Ground. If there are no spaces left you could see if Bidford Boats have any spare room, or try Barton/E&H Billington Lock which is linked by footpath to Bidford, a quarter of an hour's walk away.

Five lesiurely miles upstream of Bidford, the river splits into several channels - only one of which is navigable - to pass beneath the ancient arches of Binton Bridges. Nearby lies the trackbed of the old Stratford & Midland Junction Railway, one of those endearingly independent cross-country lines which seemed to lead from nowhere to nowhere. At plum-picking time as many as twenty wagons a day were loaded with fruit in the tiny siding at Binton. Amongst the line's best remembered trains were the banana specials operated by the Midland Railway between Avon-mouth Docks and London; a somewhat elongated route. Binton church - half a mile to the north - is worth a detour. One of its stained glass windows commemorates Captain Scott's polar expedition. The connection being that the rector's sister, Kathleen, was the explorer's wife, a well-known sculptress and, of course, the mother of naturalist, painter and early inland waterway activist, Peter Scott - see Map 34.

Bidford-on-Avon

Map 6

There is a resort-like air about Bidford. Day-trippers pour on to the riverside recreation ground but rarely stray further than the local pubs and fast food outlets. Moreover such over-indulgences fail to mar what is an otherwise attractive village. In any case, Shakespeare came here to debauch himself too, immortalising the place in one of his poems as 'drunken Bidford'.

Eating & Drinking

THE BRIDGE - High Street. Tel: 01789 773700. Stylish and popular 'eaterie'. Riverside decking and customer moorings. B50 4BG

THE COTTAGE OF CONTENT - Barton. Tel: 01789 772279. Cosy traditional pub with camping on south bank of river and Shakespeare's Avon Way. B50 4NP

Shopping

More shops than most villages of this size can sustain: butcher, bakery (with tea room) pharmacy, convenience store (with cash machine), newsagent, hardware store, and even a branch of Lloyds bank. Budgens supermarket with post office on main road.

Connections

BUSES - service X18 operates half-hourly (hourly Sun) to/from Evesham and Stratford. Tel: 0871 200 2233.

Welford-on-Avon

Map 6

Lack of public moorings prevents easy exploration of this pretty village complete with maypole, thatched cottages, convenience store and butcher who does a nice line in filled rolls, baguettes and home made pies. The FOUR ALLS at Binton Bridges (Tel: 01789 751470 - CV37 8PW) offers limited customer moorings, whilst there are two more pubs - more handy for walkers - in the village: THE BELL (Tel: 01789 750353 - CV37 8EB) and THE SHAKESPEARE (Tel: 01789 750443 - CV37 8PX). Bus 27 runs bi-hourly Mon-Sat to/from Stratford.

7 AVON NAVIGATION Stratford-on-Avon 4mls/3lks/1.5hrs*

⚠ Advice for Boaters

1. Picking up and setting down crew members at the entrance to Bancroft Basin is not easy and it may be advisable to take the long way round by Tramway Bridge.

2. Whilst the statutory head of navigation is at Alveston, 3 miles upstream of Stratford, in practice it is inadvisable for deep-draughted craft to proceed beyond Cliffe Cottage, whilst the average narrow boat will find even the Old Bathing Place potentially shallow.

Stratford Waterways Information Centre is based on a boat in Bancroft Basin. A fun of local boating knowledge, it is open daily, Apr-Oct, 9.30am-6pm. Tel: 07584 08632

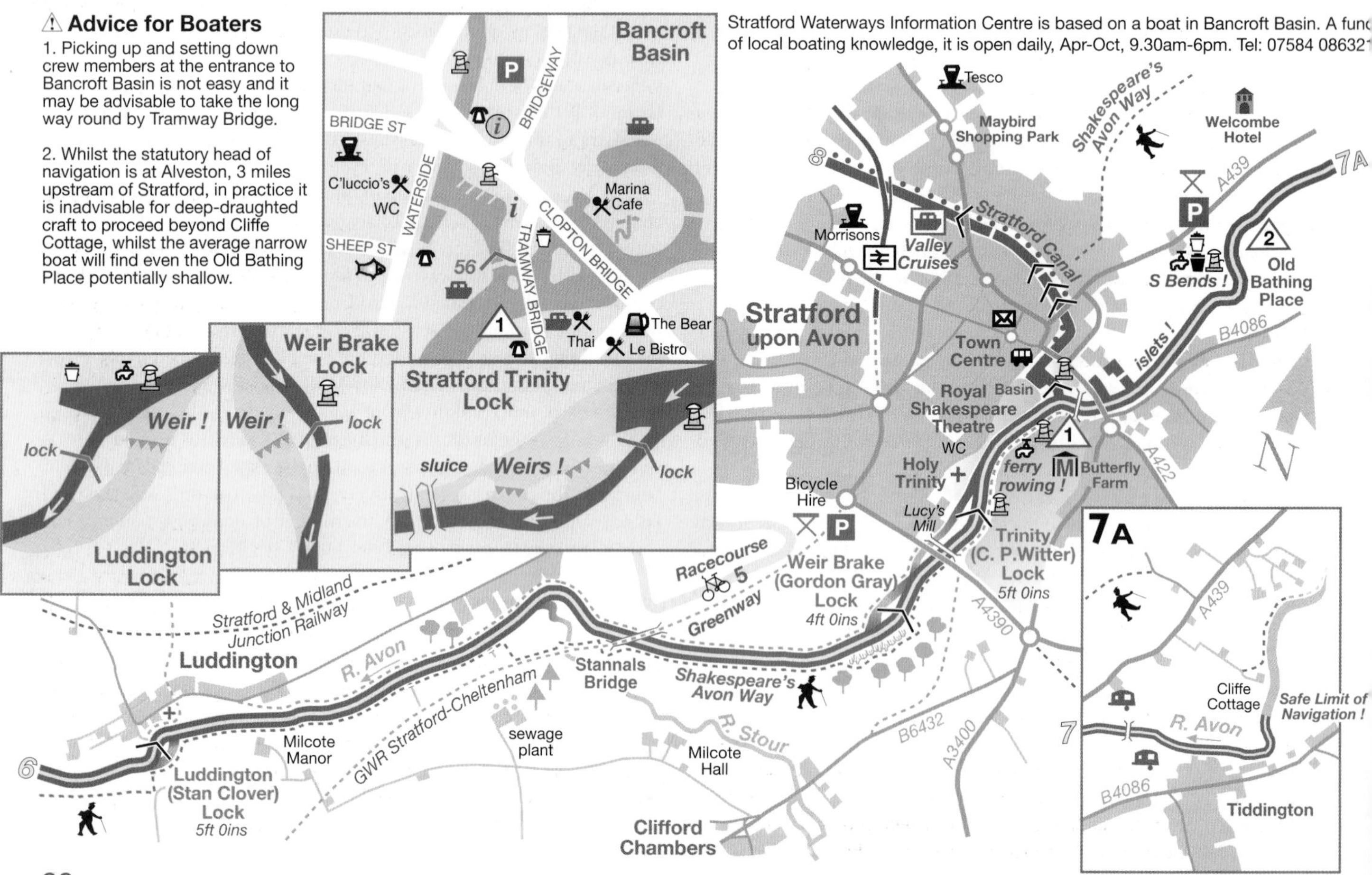

*Time refers to Luddington to Stratford and the lock count does not include access to Bancroft Basin.

BOATERS have three river locks to contend with (plus a fourth if they are moving on to or off the canal at Stratford) as the Avon winds from Luddington, past Stratford, to the present head of navigation at Alveston Weir. Luddington Lock's alternative name honours one of the former Upper Avon Navigation Trust's loyal supporters. Boosted by the Stour, whose source lies near the brewery town of Hook Norton, the Avon widens perceptibly after the narrow reaches in the vicinity of Bidford. Above the confluence a large steel girder bridge carries the trackbed of the old Great Western Railway's Stratford-Cheltenham line. Now known as 'The Greenway', it stretches from Stratford to Long Marston, a useful escape route from the busy tourist town for walkers, cyclists and horse-riders. The indefatigable Andrew Yarranton proposed rendering the Stour navigable in the 17th Century.

Weir Brake Lock (built in just thirty-eight days by Borstal boys back in the early Seventies) commemorates Gordon Gray, a previously anonymous donor who made his fortune in the diamond mines of South Africa. Shakespeare's Avon Way offers a panoramic view from high above the lock. The Queen Mother travelled from here to the next lock up by narrowboat during the opening ceremony of June 1st 1974, as celebrated in the poem *Inland Waterway* by Sir John Betjeman.

The short reach separating Weir Brake and Stratford Trinity locks is spanned by the Stratford & Midland Junction Railway bridge which was converted to carry road traffic. One of the last trains to cross over the river was the Royal Train, carrying the Queen Mother to officiate at the reopening of the Stratford Canal in 1964. Her Royal Highness obviously had a weakness for Stratford and its inland waterways. A footbridge also crosses the river at this point, making it easy for pedestrians to enjoy a circular walk beside the Avon. Blocks of highly desirable flats occupy the site of Lucy's Mill, which stood here for hundreds of years and was an important customer of the river barges until the advent of the railway.

Stratford Trinity Lock is also known as Colin P. Witter Lock. Indeed, his name appears on the massive steel frames which protect the chamber from collapse threatened by high ground pressures. The bold steeple of Holy Trinity Church (Shakespeare's burial place) overlooks the lock, above which Stratford's passenger ferry boat operates by means of a submerged chain fed through a winch on the pontoon wound by the ferryman.

Stratford's riverfront is familiar to people from all over the world, though it has subtly altered since the multi-million pound refurbishment of the Royal Shakespeare Theatre, completed in 2010. As a boater, you have your own cameo role to play - just don't make too much of a performance of it! *Everyone* seems determined to get afloat, and barnacle-encrusted navigators of the Avon Ring have to keep a weather-eye peeled for sudden unexpected and unpremeditated lurches to port or starboard; whilst, after all the day-trippers have departed, the reach becomes a training ground for the more accomplished performers of Stratford Rowing Club. A long river bank, backed by a recreation ground, and excellent for mooring alongside (fee payable April to October), extends beyond the lock.

Upstream of the entrance lock to the Stratford Canal and Bancroft Basin the river is spanned by the Tramway Bridge, a redbrick structure built in 1826 to carry the Stratford & Moreton Horse Tramway. It is now used by pedestrians. In contrast, the stone arches of Clopton Bridge date back to 1480. But the two bridges harmonise well with their shared environment, as though the gap of four centuries in their age was just a twinkling ripple in the timespan of the river beneath them.

Beyond Stratford it is feasible for most craft to voyage a further mile or so to the Old Bathing Place, a picnic site provided with boating facilities, albeit on the shallow side for narrowboaters. The Stratford & Warwick Waterways Trust advocate a bold scheme to extend navigation up to a junction with the Grand Union Canal at Warwick. Six locks and a lift seem modest by the standards of many inland waterway project proposals, and the boost to tourism and the benefits of improved flood control are manifest, but the concept has so far foundered on the reactionary response of riparian landowners. Meanwhile, thanks to the continued work of ANT and its volunteers, boaters have fifty miles of gorgeous river to play with. Attitudes and personalities change - the river can bide its time.

Stratford-on-Avon Maps 7 & 8

That Stratford-on-Avon is second only to London in the esteem of foreign visitors, serves to emphasise the charisma surrounding Shakespeare. Without his omnipresence, one imagines Stratford's position in the league table of tourism would be academic. And yet, subtract the Shakespeare factor, and you are still left with an attractive town with a generous helping of good architecture, its setting enhanced by the proximity of the Avon; and there is a hair-down demeanour about the people in the streets which becomes infectious. All those earnest foreign crocodiles! Contriving a dramatic analogy, Stratford delivers its lines and plays its part with its integrity and dignity intact, really being the rather nice place to visit as extolled by the tourist propaganda.

Eating & Drinking

To eat aboard or not to eat aboard? That is the question! Sometimes Stratford's culinary options can be a tad overwhelming and it's a relief to retreat to your boat and raise the gang-plank. On the other, Hamletian hand, your crew may feel they deserve a treat, and on Sheep Street alone you'll encounter a cosmopolitan cornucopia of establishments, far too numerous to list here. Notable highlights elsewhere in the town include:

THE BEAR - Swans Nest Lane. Tel: 01789 265540. Smart, *Good Beer Guide* listed bar in the Swan's Nest Hotel. Wide choice of real ales and good menu. CV37 7LT

CARLUCCIO'S - Waterside. Tel: 01789 267424. Italian cafe/restaurant/deli overlooking basin. CV37 6BA

HATHAWAY TEA ROOMS - High Street. Tel: 01789 264022. Delightfully old-fashioned breakfasts, lunches and teas in half-timbered town centre setting. CV37 6AU

LE BISTROT PIERRE - Swans Nest Lane. Tel: 01789 264804. Stylishly appointed French restaurant. CV37 7LT

MARINA CAFE BISTRO - Clopton Bridge. Tel: 01789 299921. Friendly waterside eatery. CV37 6YY

ROOFTOP - Royal Shakespeare Theatre. Tel: 01789 403449. Open daily from 11.30am for lunch, drinks and dinner. CV37 6BB

THAI BOATHOUSE - riverside between Tramway and Clopton bridges. Tel: 01789 297733. Thai restaurant housed in elegant timber boathouse. CV37 7LS

Shopping

Market day is Friday and a good one it is too; plus Farmers' Markets on the first and third Saturdays of the month and craft markets on the second and fourth Saturdays. Elsewhere the town bristles with quality shops engaged in the hectic business of emptying the bank accounts of visitors. But many of these shops have such character that you don't resent being plunged into the red. The best policy, chaps, is to get here after the shops have shut and insist on an early start. On the northern outskirts of town, within easy reach of Bridge 65 on the Stratford Canal, lies Maybird Shopping Park.

Things to Do

TOURIST INFORMATION - Bridgefoot. Tel: 01789 264293. 9am-5pm (10am-4pm Suns). CV37 6GW

ROYAL SHAKESPEARE THEATRE - Waterside. Whatever else you do in Stratford, try to catch a performance at the RST. Tel: 0844 800 1110. CV37 6BB

SHAKESPEARE'S BIRTHPLACE - Henley Street. Tel: 01789 293455. S's childhood home. Additionally the custodians of four other properties in the district. CV37 6QW

CITY SIGHTSEEING - Open top bus tours providing a good introduction to the town. Tel: 01789 412680.

SHAKESPEARE EXPRESS - Tel: 0121 708 4960. The Bard's favourite means of transport - steam hauled trains to Birmingham and back on Sundays July-mid Sep.

AVON-BOATING - Swan's Nest. Tel: 01789 267073. Skiff, punt and motor-boat hire, plus river trips. CV37 7LS

TRADITIONAL CYCLE SHOP - Clopton Bridge. Tel: 01789 290703. Hire, sales & servicing. CV37 6YY

Connections

BUSES - useful downriver links with Bidford-on-Avon and Evesham (Stagecoach X18) and up-canal connections with Wootton Wawen, Hockley Heath, Shirley et al (Johnson's Excelbus X20). Tel: 0871 200 2233.

TRAINS - half-hourly London Midland services to Birmingham. Less frequent but useful direct link with London Marylebone by Chiltern Trains. Parkway station open adjacent Stratford Canal Bridge 63. Tel: 03457 484950.

TAXIS - Stratford Taxis. Tel: 01789 414007.

Wilmcote Map 8

MARY ARDEN'S FARM (Tel: 01789 293455 - CV37 9UN) is the cynosure of this commuter village, formerly a centre for quarrying. Otherwise of note is the Anglo-Catholic church by Butterfield. Two pubs provide refreshments: the MASON'S ARMS (Tel: 01789 297416 - CV39 9XX) and MARY ARDEN INN (Tel: 01789 267030 - CV39 9XJ); and the convenience store opens daily. Trains run hourly, daily to/from Stratford.

Wootton Wawen Map 9

Wootton Hall is a 17th century mansion which once belonged to Maria Fitzherbert, the *secret* wife of George IV. The parish church is of Saxon origin and considered one of Warwickshire's finest.

THE NAVIGATION - canalside by the aqueduct. Tel: 01564 792676. Bar and restaurant meals. B95 6BZ

YEW TREE FARM - Tel: 01564 792701. Barns and byres transformed into a 'contemporary shopping village'. Farm shop & coffee shop. B95 6BY

General stores in the centre of the village and post office in side building of Wootton Hall.

BUSES - Johnson's service X20 runs hourly Mon-Sat and slightly less frequently on Suns to/from Birmingham via Hockley Heath and Stratford. Tel: 0871 200 2233.

TRAINS - hourly service (ex Suns) to/from Birmingham and Stratford. Tel: 03457 484950.

Stratford Canal

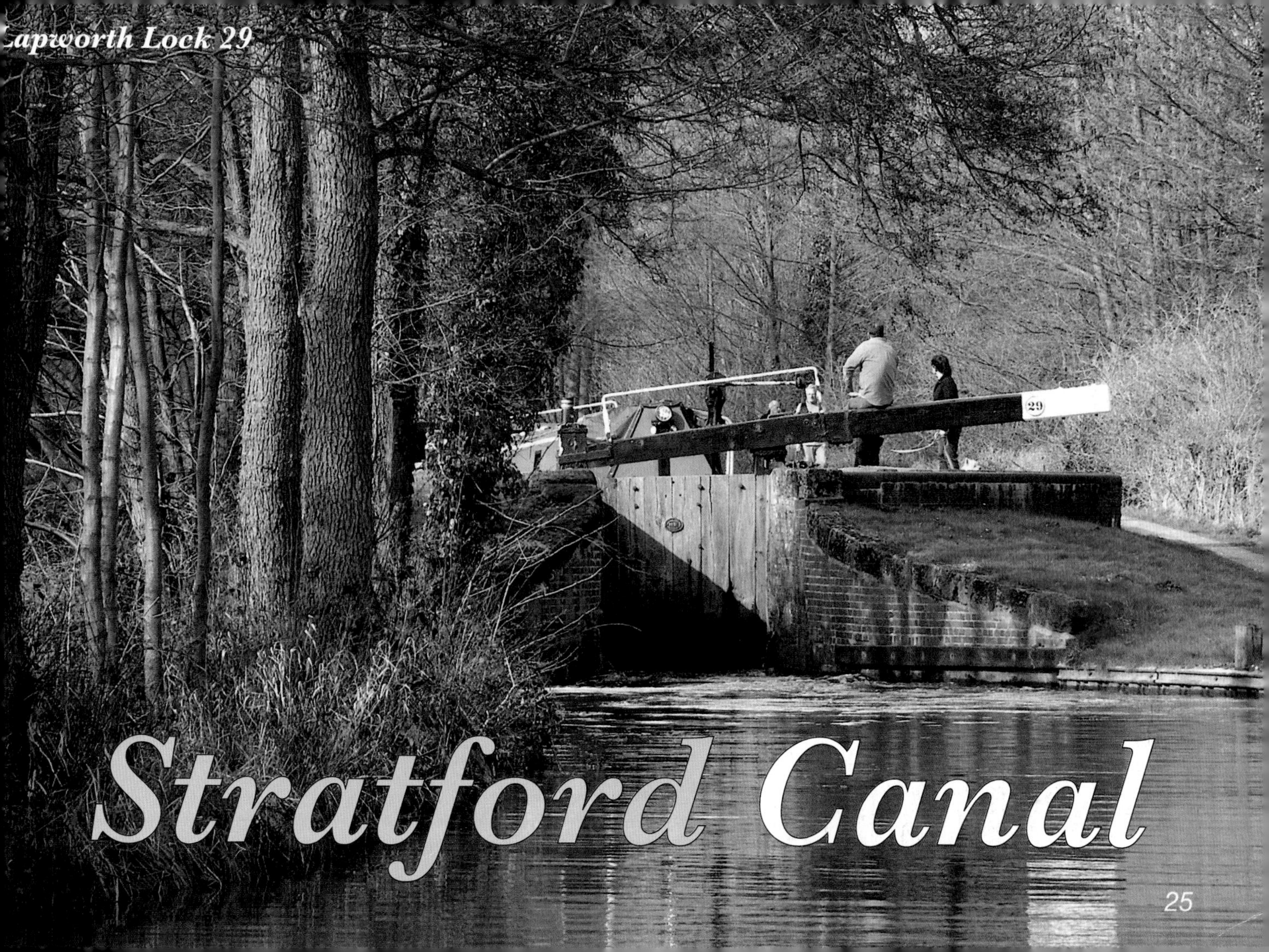

Lapworth Lock 29

8 STRATFORD CANAL Stratford-on-Avon 4mls/17lks/4hrs

WHEN, on a walk back from Wilmcote to see Mary Arden's House, an impressionable, adolescent Robert Aickman encountered the decay which the hitherto unimpeachable Great Western Railway had indifferently permitted to fall upon the Stratford Canal, it instilled in him an affection for lost causes generally - and canals in particular - which years later prompted the formation of the Inland Waterways Association. And it is this selfsame Stratford Canal which holds a special place in the affections of a generation of canal enthusiasts, its southern section being the first great restoration success of the post-war canal movement. It was transformed from virtual dereliction and the threat of abandonment in 1958 to navigable status once again in 1964. The restoration project, managed by the indomitable David Hutchings, was undertaken under the aegis of the National Trust, but in 1988 ownership of the canal passed to British Waterways and now, of course, the Canal & River Trust.

Once a centre for transhipment of cargoes, commercial activity at Bancroft Basin these days is confined to ice cream boats, baguette boats, and a floating art gallery. Usefully, the Avon Navigation Trust and the Canal & River Trust have clubbed together in the provision of a floating information centre; somewhere to get hold of each organisation's licences if you haven't already got one.

It is an entertaining spot to moor; however, always assuming you are gregariously predisposed and able to find space in the fishbone moorings. Quieter canal moorings are to be had through Bridge 69, an unobtrusive exit from the basin which begins (or, of course, ends) exploration of the Stratford Canal, and the canal's traverse of the town's eastern outskirts, through a quartet of locks, is surprisingly anonymous; a Rosencrantz and Guildenstern kind of canal.

Above the locks, Valley Cruises boatyard and hire base creates a sense of activity as the canal passes beneath two railway bridges - look out for Summer Sunday steam trains. Well kept and easy to operate, Wilmcote Locks are divided into three distinct parts: two outer threes and a middle five. For ease of maintenance and access to two canalside cottages, the status of the towpath here has been upgraded to that of a minor road.

Bridge 59 was the straw that almost broke the camel's back. Its deterioration caused the local authority to seek permission to abandon the canal back in 1958, so that they could divert the roadway across the bed of the waterway. Evidence as to the canal's use relied on the purchase of a solitary ticket for a canoe trip the previous year! The canal narrows at the site of a former quarry and lime-burning wharf, and the abutments of an old tramway bridge recall this activity.

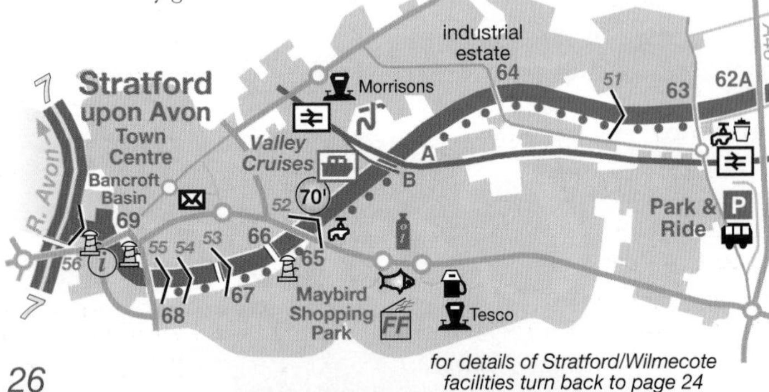

The Stratford Canal's towpath is in excellent condition all the way up to Wilmcote beyond which, though wide, it is inclined to be a bit bumpy for all but the most firm-bottomed and stoic of cyclists.

for details of Stratford/Wilmecote facilities turn back to page 24

9 STRATFORD CANAL Wootton Wawen 3.5mls/1lk/1.5hrs

BESIDES being so long in the building*, the Stratford Canal never attracted as much trade as its dewy-eyed promoters envisaged. Lacking a hinterland of heavy industry, its main traffic might have been manufactured goods from Birmingham and the Black Country destined for export from Bristol, but the Avon was ponderous in comparison with the virile Severn, so most of that business went down the Worcester & Birmingham. Volume peaked in 1838 at 180,000 tons, and within twenty years the canal had been sold to one of the fledgling railway companies, the Oxford, Worcester & Wolverhampton, itself absorbed by the Great Western in 1865, hence the lozenge weight-restriction notices still encountered as you make your way along the canal.

Bearley (or rather more romantically, Odd) Lock separates two lengthy and delightfully remote pounds between the locks at Wilmcote and Preston Bagot. The Warwickshire countryside is at its loveliest and the canal offers wide vistas over rolling hills. Edstone Aqueduct is, without question, the Stratford Canal's most dramatic engineering feature. It consists of an iron trough resting on thirteen tapering brick piers. At 28 feet high and 475 feet long, it seems modest enough, but in the context of the gently undulating landscape, its sudden appearance has the majesty and startling effect of the renowned Pontcysyllte Aqueduct on the Llangollen Canal. The sunken towpath offers walkers a strange, fish-eye lens view of passing boaters. The aqueduct spans a by-road, a tributary of the River Alne and the twin tracks of the Birmingham & North Warwickshire Railway. Those with a highly-developed railway eye will notice an overgrown trackbed curving away from beneath the aqueduct across the countryside in a north-westerly direction. This was the Great Western Railway's Alcester branch, an ill-fated and relatively shortlived line which had its track lifted as an economy measure during the First World War, re-opened in 1923, then closed again at the beginning of the Second World War, apart from a cloak and dagger service operated for employees at a motor works evacuated from Coventry. A Heath Robinsonish arrangement of pipes and valves enabled steam locomotives on the branch to take on canal water directly beneath the aqueduct.

Wootton Wawen Aqueduct is a more modest affair than Edstone, but it fights a running battle with juggernauts on the A34. On several occasions it has borne the brunt of high-sided vehicles whose drivers' sense of spacial awareness left something to be desired. Nevertheless, it has stood its ground since 1813 and should be good for a few years yet.

The majority of bridges on this section of the canal are of the charmingly delicate split-cantilever design peculiar to the Stratford. The narrow gap between the two cast-iron arches was designed to permit the tow rope to pass. Compatriot and friend of Rachmaninov, the exiled composer, Nikolai Medtner (1880-1951) and his wife lived on the western outskirts of Wootton Wawen during the Second World War as a guest of the pianist, Edna Iles and her parents. Inspired by the local countryside, his Third Piano Concerto was completed here and premiered at The Proms in 1943.

*see Map 11

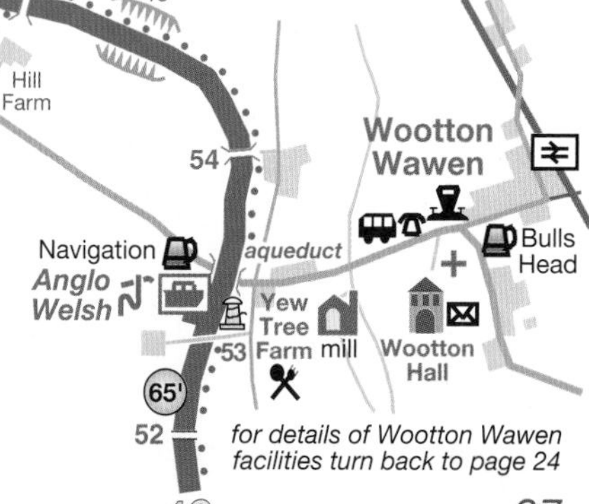

10 STRATFORD CANAL Lowsonford 5mls/13lks/4hrs

LOSING itself in the last vestiges of the old Forest of Arden, the canal assumes an ethereal quality; one anticipates encountering Rosalind and Orlando at any moment. From Preston Bagot to Lowsonford - plotting a lonely course across Yarningale Common, and coming upon Yarningale Aqueduct, the baby of the Stratford Canal family - you are hard-pressed to recall a prettier canal, rendering associations with Shakespeare's heroine, all the more appropriate.The barrel-roofed cottages by locks 34 and 37 have been incorporated into modern extensions, but those by locks 28 and 31 remain largely unspoilt. The latter belongs now to the Landmark Trust* and is available for holiday hire. An Antony (Angel of the North) Gormley sculpture briefly presided over the lock in 2015 to celebrate the Trust's 50th Anniversary. The design of these cottages is said to have resulted from the use of the same wooden frames used in the construction of the brick road bridges which span the canal.

The abutments of a former railway bridge frame the canal near Lowsonford. The bridge carried a branch-line to Henley-in-Arden, closed when the route was made obsolete by the opening of the North Warwickshire Railway. Legend has it that the track was despatched to The Front during the Great War but ended up at the bottom of the English Channel: *malheureusement,* it seems unlikely that the M40 will be as shortlived.

Woods border the canal, birdsong fills the air, the scent of wildflowers is intoxicating. Temple Thurston was equally taken with this part of the Stratford Canal. In 1910 he hired a narrowboat known as *The Flower of Gloster*, its captain Eynsham Harry, together with a horse called Fanny and set off on a journey of discovery which has remained a 'desert island' favourite of many canal enthusiasts ever since. Temple Thurston described the Stratford Canal as being 'right out of the track of the world'. He climbed the hillside to a farm at Yarningale for fresh milk, and Eynsham Harry bought beer from the wife of a lock-keeper. Simple joys long vanished, though you can follow the footpath westwards from Bridge 46 to visit Preston Bagot's lonely little church. A brass memorial, dated 1637, marks the resting place of Elisabeth Randoll: five centuries in a flash!

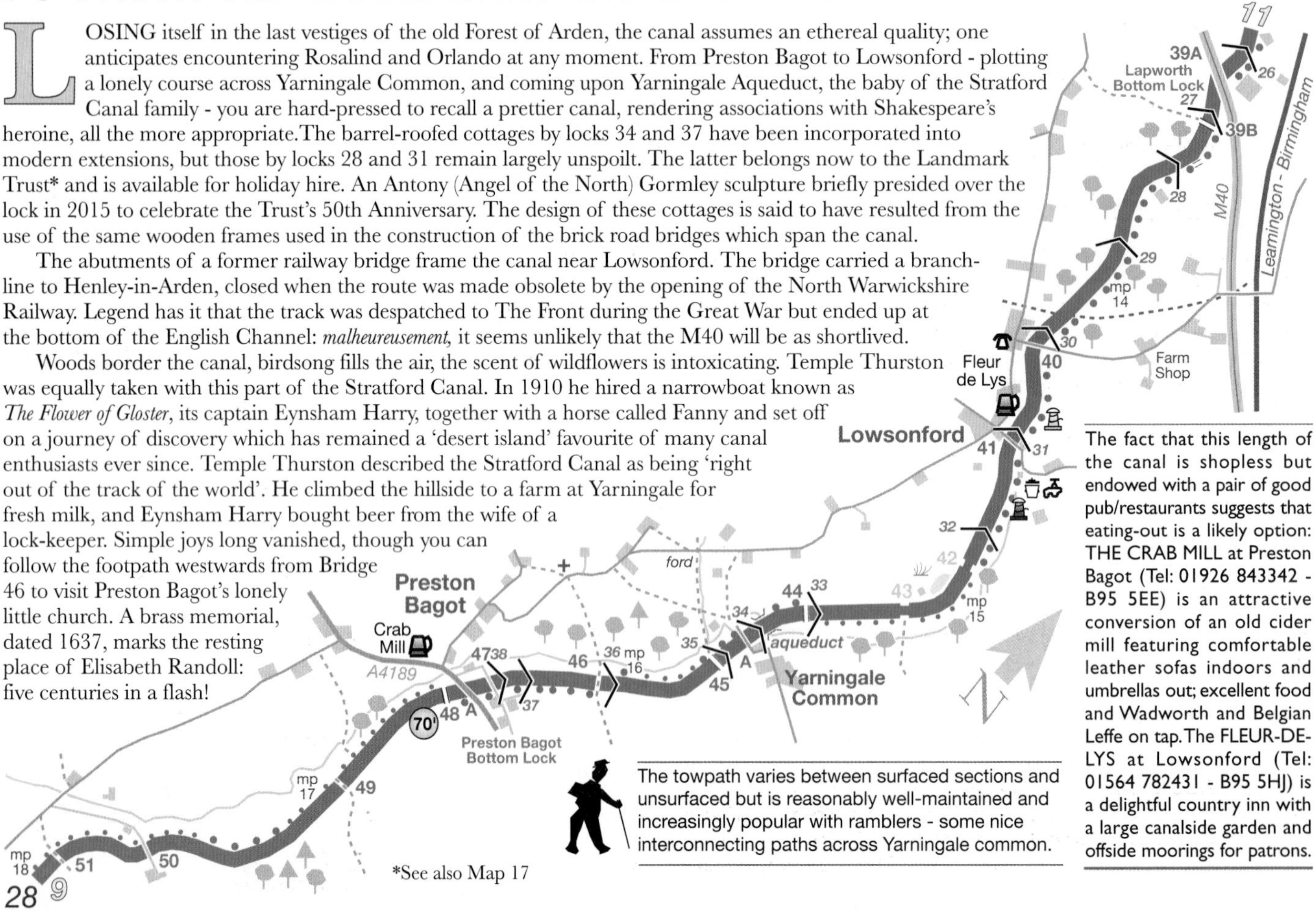

The towpath varies between surfaced sections and unsurfaced but is reasonably well-maintained and increasingly popular with ramblers - some nice interconnecting paths across Yarningale common.

The fact that this length of the canal is shopless but endowed with a pair of good pub/restaurants suggests that eating-out is a likely option: THE CRAB MILL at Preston Bagot (Tel: 01926 843342 - B95 5EE) is an attractive conversion of an old cider mill featuring comfortable leather sofas indoors and umbrellas out; excellent food and Wadworth and Belgian Leffe on tap.The FLEUR-DE-LYS at Lowsonford (Tel: 01564 782431 - B95 5HJ) is a delightful country inn with a large canalside garden and offside moorings for patrons.

*See also Map 17

11 STRATFORD CANAL Kingswood Jnct. 4mls/23lks/5hrs

WHETHER you arrive by boat, by bike, or on foot - and however many times you have been there before - Kingswood Junction never fails to captivate. Either side of the junction, the Stratford Canal's unremitting locks can tax the boater, so there is every motive for pausing here, and soaking up the scene. Certainly there is much to see, and the configuration of the two briefly parallel canals, together with the connecting arm, provides plenty of opportunities for circular or figure-of-eight strolls. A car park and picnic area, well masked by pine trees, encourage the non-boat-owning or hiring public to come to the junction, whilst the proximity of Lapworth railway station is serendipitously advantageous for those environmentally conscientious enough to favour the use of public transport.

A short branch canal was built between the Warwick & Birmingham Canal (as the Grand Union was previously called) and the Stratford-on-Avon Canal in 1802. It became a bone of contention between the two companies, jealous of each other's traffics and water supplies. Such emnities are long forgotten, and now the branch provides a strategic link between two popular cruising routes. The lower of two small reservoirs has been adapted for long term moorings, the upper is used by anglers. Hail them with a hearty 'well done', they look like they are only fishing for compliments.

South of Kingswood the Stratford Canal continues its ascent from, or descent to, the Avon. There are barrel-roofed cottages by locks 21 and 25. The latter was the home, for many years, of Doug Smith, celebrated cartographer of the canals, whose meticulously drawn 'Lockmaster' pen & ink maps of the system adorn many an enthusiast's wall. Doug was a ferroequinologist too, and relished the propinquity of both transport modes to his home. A wooden bench by Bridge 39 fittingly commemorates his contribution to the canals.

The most dramatic section of the Lapworth flight lies between bridges 32 and 33, beyond Kingswood Junction on the northern section of the Stratford Canal. Here there are seven chambers in close proximity, presenting a spectacular view irrespective of whether you are looking up or down. Leaving Kingswood for King's Norton there are eighteen locks to negotiate before reaching the summit. The top lock is numbered'2' because the guillotine stop lock at Kings Norton (Map 13) was considered to be No.1.

Just to add variety, bridges 26 and 28 are lifting structures: the former of Llangollen pattern; the latter reminiscent of those found in profusion on the Oxford Canal ... both are windlass-operated. A winding-hole by Bridge 27 marks the temporary terminus of the canal between 1796 and 1800, an hiatus brought about by lack of capital. It took so long to build this canal that it averaged little more than a mile a year. The engineer was Josiah Clowes.

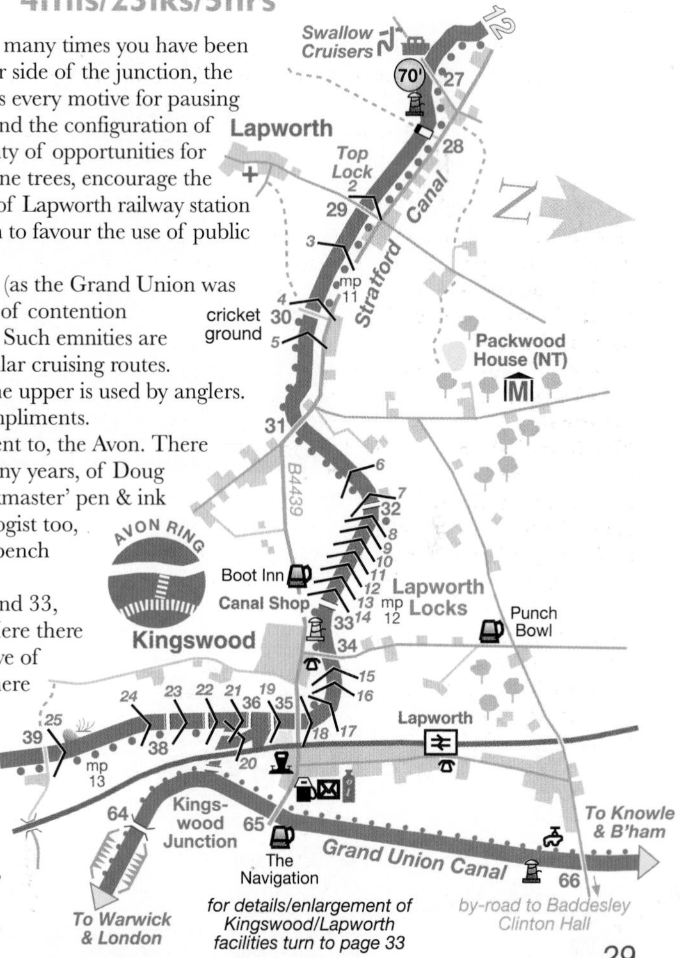

for details/enlargement of Kingswood/Lapworth facilities turn to page 33

Stratford Canal

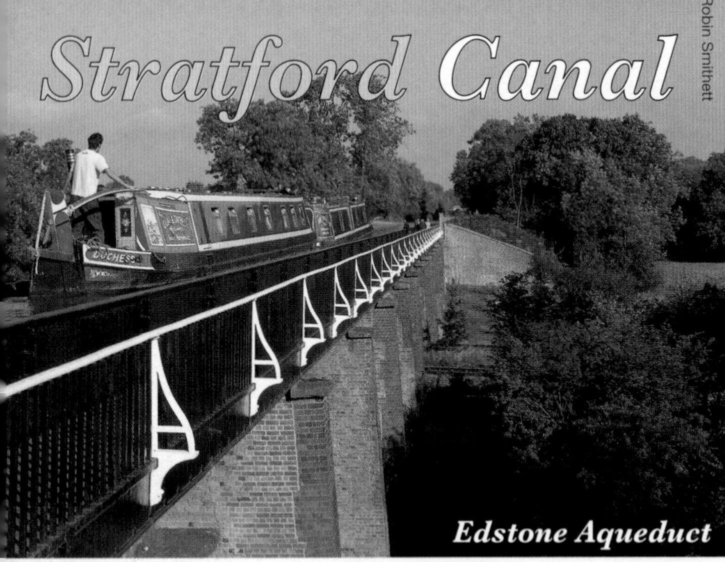

Robin Smithett

Edstone Aqueduct

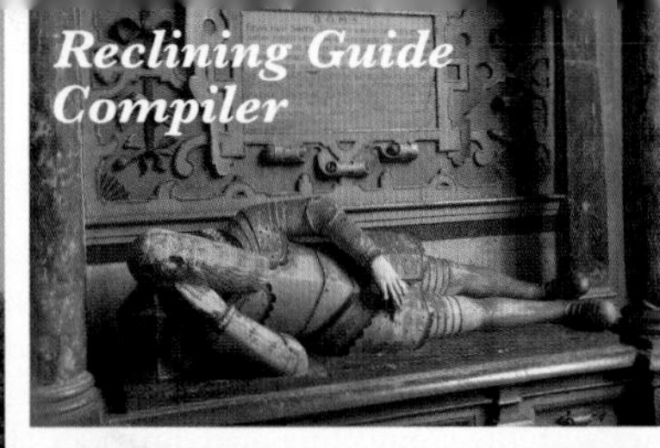

Reclining Guide Compiler

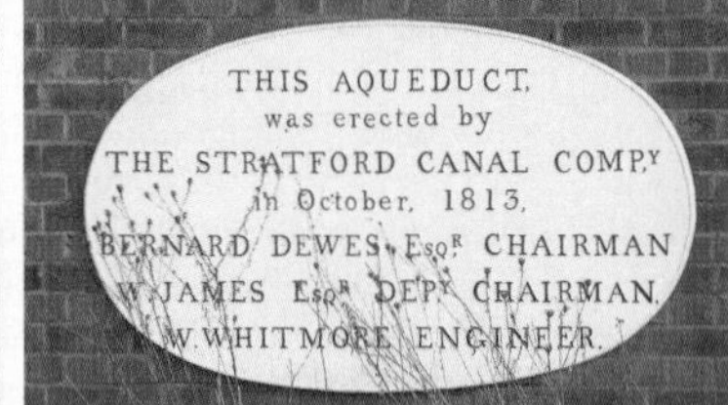

Lock 21

Lock 20

'Lock 1'

Wootton Wawen

Preston Bagot

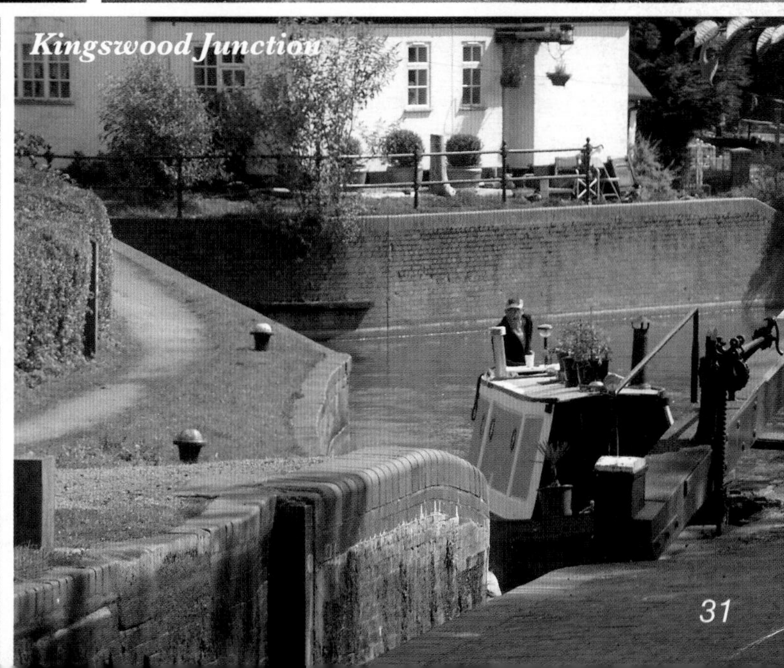
Kingswood Junction

Hockley Heath

12 STRATFORD CANAL Hockley Heath 5mls/0lks/2hrs

FREE from locks, the northern section of the Stratford Canal saunters around the suburban fringes of Birmingham largely impervious to their existence. Its hinterland, however, seldom lacks interest. From the visitor moorings at Hockley Heath by Bridge 25, you can make your way past an imposing Victorian Baptist church (built of blue lias) to the Nuthurst obelisk raised in 1749 by Thomas Archer - architect of St Philip's Cathedral in Birmingham - to modestly mark his elevation to the peerage.

Much of the canal is tree-lined. Oak, alder, hazel and willow predominate, creating a soothing, sylvan quality which, however beautiful, is apt to become soporific after a while. When you do catch glimpses of the surrounding countryside, it reminds you of the Home Counties, exuding an air of affluence epitomised by large detached houses, and horsey people, trotting down dappled lanes on dappled steeds.

The winding hole by Bridge 22 marks the site of a wharf once linked by tramway to the limestone quarries of Tanworth-in-Arden. Originally a branch canal had been planned to cater for this traffic. Near Bridge 19 the extensive, but private miniature railway of the Birmingham Society of Model Engineers stands close to the canal, though hidden by a cutting. It does, however, open to the public on selected dates.

St Patrick's Church by Bridge 17 at Salter Street, was built with money paid by the canal company in compensation for acquiring common land on which to built Earlswood Reservoirs. An embankment carries the canal over Spring Brook and a feeder enters the canal from the reservoirs which lie to the south-west. These days they are a popular amenity, attracting ramblers, anglers, bird watchers and interpretive board collectors. Looking a bit sorry for itself now, the old engine house, to which narrowboats carried coal up the feeder until 1936, could usefully be refurbished as a small museum of social and natural local history. Earlswood Motor Yacht Club members use the feeder now for moorings and offer various boating facilities together with meals at their club house.

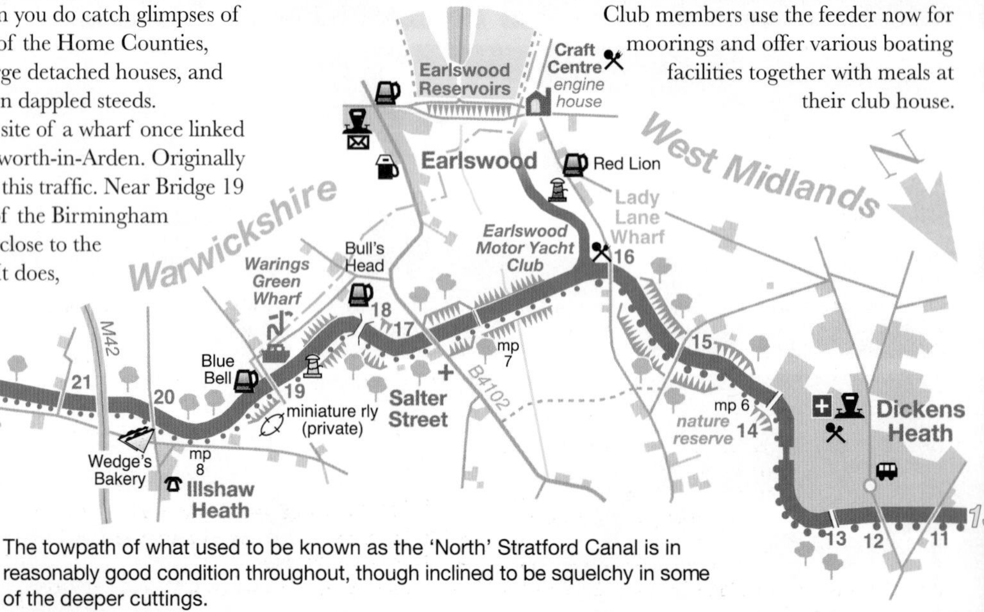

The towpath of what used to be known as the 'North' Stratford Canal is in reasonably good condition throughout, though inclined to be squelchy in some of the deeper cuttings.

Kingswood/Lapworth Map 11

Twin villages in North Warwickshire's commuter belt where the property prices routinely run into seven figures. On kind days there is no more pleasant an activity than to sit on one of the benches overlooking the reservoirs, idly watching boats, trains and people go by. St Mary's church, reached by a field path from Bridge 30 or by road from Bridge 29, is a gem, curiously equipped with a detached tower and a chantry atop an open archway. Inside there is a stained glass window dedicated to a victim of the First World War, and a memorial tablet by Eric Gill. In the churchyard there's a tomb belonging to the Catesby family of Gunpowder Plot infamy. Lapworth Cricket Club, founded 1908, has a picturesque ground alongside the Stratford Canal between locks 4 and 5. Dr Johnson's parents were married at nearby Packwood's church in 1706.

Eating & Drinking

THE BOOT - adjacent Bridge 33 (Stratford Canal). Tel: 01564 782464. Gastro-pub. B93 0EB

THE NAVIGATION - canalside Bridge 65 (Grand Union). Tel: 01564 783337. Traditional country pub offering a good choice of real ales and bar, restaurant and take-away food. B94 6NA

Shopping

Village shop by railway bridge between the canals. Off licence/post office by Bridge 65 (Grand Union). Gifts, and canalia (not to mention home made cakes) from the BRIAR COTTAGE canal shop by Bridge 33 - Tel: 01564 782379.

Things to Do

BADDESLEY CLINTON HALL (B93 0DQ) and PACKWOOD HOUSE (B94 6AT) are National Trust properties within easy reach of either canal. The former is a romantic medieval manor house hidden in Arden woodland, the latter a Tudor building with a celebrated formal yew garden said to represent the Sermon on the Mount. NT gift shops at both houses; restaurant at former only. Contact 01564 783294/782024 for full details of opening times etc.

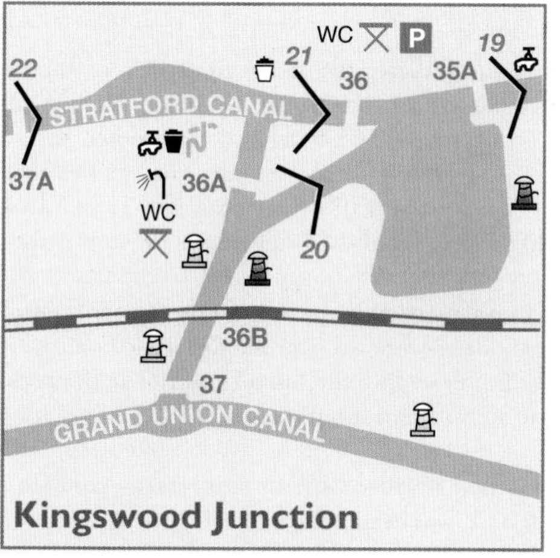

Connections

TRAINS - approx bi-hourly Chiltern Trains service linking with Warwick, Leamington, Birmingham Moor Street/Snow Hill and Marylebone. Tel: 08457 484950.

Hockley Heath Map 12

Rendering the Stratford road's traffic subliminal, will aid enjoyment of what this suburban community has to offer. Take in the triangular, pillared war memorial with its sundial and poignant inscription: "The days short, the work great, their time passed like a shadow"; or admire the hefty arts & crafts memorial hall dedicated to George VI.

Eating & Drinking

WHARF TAVERN - canalside Bridge 25. Tel: 01564 782075. Carvery meals and waterside garden overlooking stub of old wharf. B94 6QT

There's also a fish & chip shop, Chinese takeaway, Indian restaurant and steak bar.

Shopping

Convenience store and post office on one side of Bridge 25, delicatessen and butcher on the other.

Connections

BUSES - service X20 usefully links Hockley Heath hourly Mon-Sat with Birmingham, Henley-in-Arden and Stratford-on-Avon. Tel: 0871 200 2233.

Illshaw Heath Map 12

Wedge's wonderful bakery (Tel: 01564 702542 - B94 6RP) flourishes in its unlikely rural setting in the shadow of the M42. Fresh bread, sandwiches made to order, pies in profusion, mouthwatering cakes and puddings and a vegetable stall make it difficult for passing canaller's to resist. Outdoor tables beneath a canopy for immediate consumption.

By Bridge 19, the BLUE BELL (Tel: 01564 702328 - B94 6BP) is a rare cider house, though beer and food are also available.

Earlswood Map 12

BULL'S HEAD on Lime Kiln Lane is a charming country pub with a good choice of food (Tel: 01564 702335 - B94 6BU) and you can say the same for the RED LION a quarter of a mile south of Bridge 16 (Tel: 01564 702325 - B94 6AQ).

Dickens Heath Map 12

Trumpeted as a 'village for the 21st Century', anything less like a village than Dickens Heath would be difficult to imagine. Balconied apartments - which wouldn't look out of place in Fuerteventura - overlook the nonplussed canal, and though there are shops and restaurants in there somewhere, we wouldn't advise you to go too far in search of them, lest you get irretrievably stranded in the future.

13 STRATFORD CANAL King's Norton 5mls/0lks/2hrs

ALTHOUGH the map emphasises how built-up these south-western suburbs of Birmingham are, the canal seems oblivious to the proximity of so many houses and people, retaining an aloof quality, like a recluse in a crowd. The boater's steady progress is interrupted by having to throttle down past moored boats at the bottom of gardens. Another obstacle to progress is Shirley Drawbridge, an electrified lift bridge on a busyish by-road, necessitating the use of barriers accessed with a Canal & River Trust Yale key. Wake Green Amateurs football club's sloping pitches abut the lift bridge. South of Bridge 5 are the impressive premises of Yardley Wood Bus Garage.

Wool-gathering between sonnets, Shakespeare looks inscrutably down from the western portal of Brandwood Tunnel. Brandwood was built without a towpath, so horses were led over the top while boats were worked through by the simple expedient of boatmen pulling on a handrail set into the tunnel lining. The horse path still provides walkers with a right of way and also offers access to some useful suburban shops. Sometimes it's good to go 'over the top'.

Between the tunnel and King's Norton Junction stood a bridge with a history, a *cause celebre* in the embryonic days of the Inland Waterways Association. It was originally a lift bridge and, during the Second World War the Great Western Railway, who owned the canal at that time, clamped down the platform following damage by a lorry. Commercial traffic had ceased on the canal, but the IWA maintained that a right of navigation still applied. The GWR claimed that they would be only too happy to jack up the bridge to permit boats to pass as required, little realising that the IWA intended to organise as many boat passages as would be necessary to have the bridge fully repaired. Several campaign cruises ensued, but it was not until Nationalisation that a fully operable swing bridge was installed. Often erroneously referred to as Lifford Lane Bridge, Bridge 2 was, in fact on, Tunnel Lane. Long disused, the 'guillotine' stop lock at Bridge 1 was officially Lock No.1.

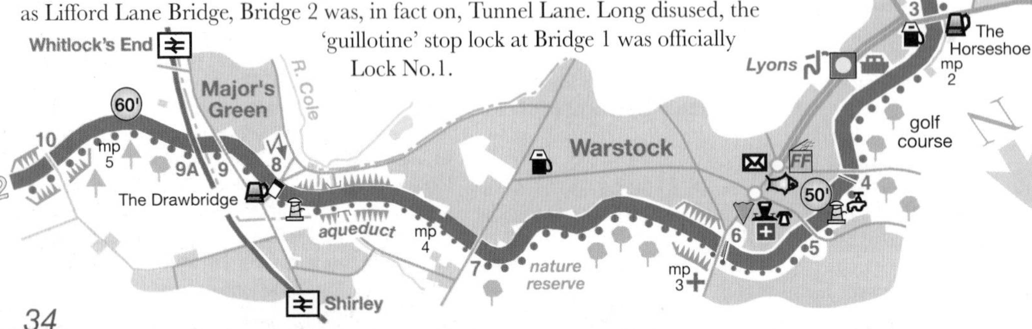

Summary of Facilities

WARSTOCK'S useful facilities, including Co-op, post office, newsagent, greengrocer, butcher, pharmacy, McDonald's, Chinese t/a and a fish & chip shop, are just a short walk south from Bridge 5, where visitor moorings and a water point are provided. Above Brandwood Tunnel you'll find a convenience store, a fish & chip shop and a sandwich shop/cafe which will take advance orders on 0121 444 004. There's a pair of canalside pubs: The Drawbridge by Bridge 8 (Tel: 0121 474 5904 - B90 1DD); and The Horseshoe by Bridge 3 (Tel: 0121 441 1661 - B14 5EL).

Worcester & Birmingham

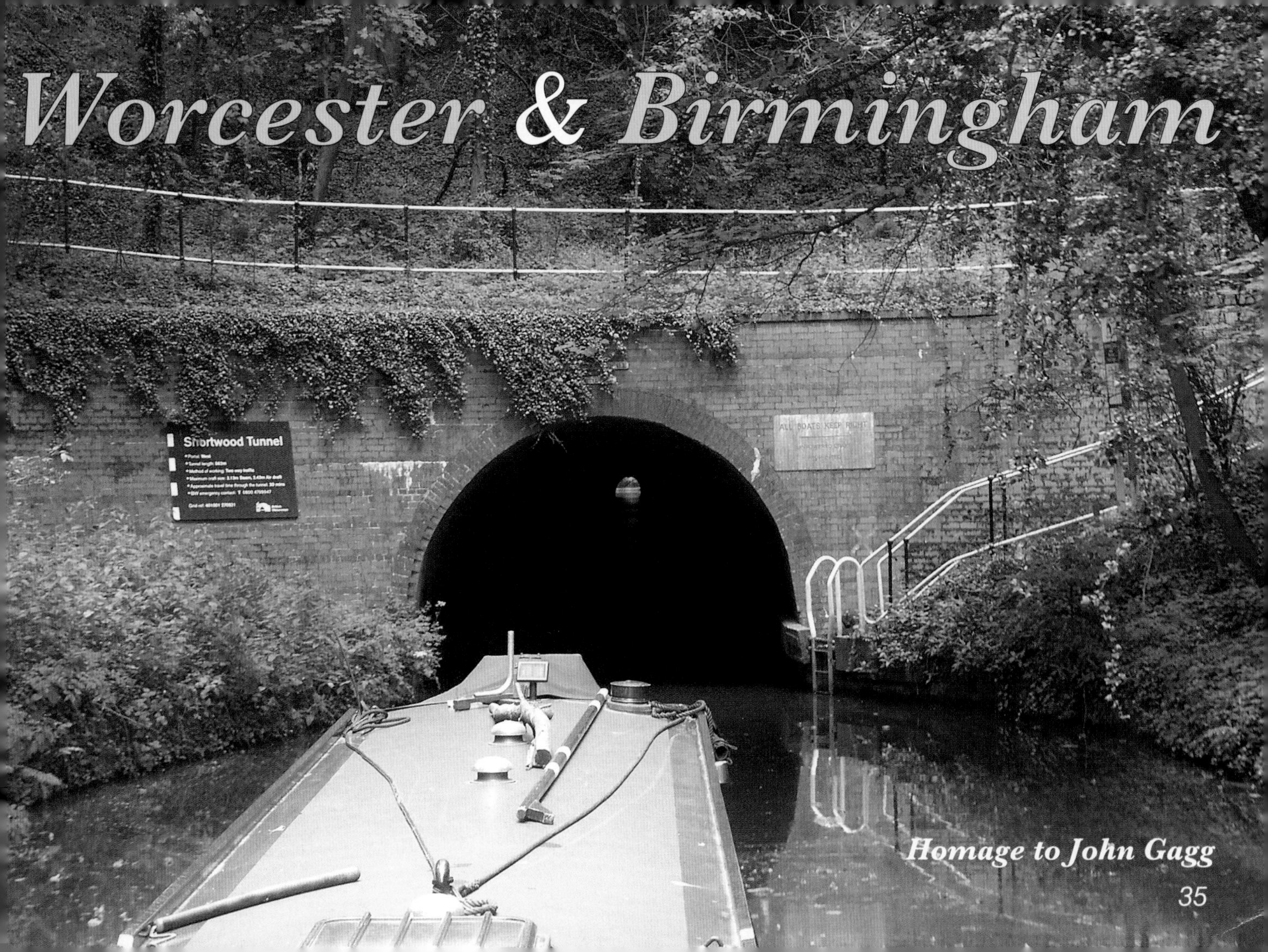

Homage to John Gagg

14 WORCESTER & BIRMINGHAM CANAL Birmingham 4mls/0lks/1.5hrs

OLD TURN JUNCTION might well be described as the pivotal point of the inland waterways network. Overlooked by the Barclaycard Arena and Sea Life Centre, it symbolises the massive changes which have overtaken the canals generally - and those of Birmingham and the Black Country in particular - during the last decade or two. All a far cry from the day, over two centuries ago, when a certain Mr Farmer's land was bisected by the new fangled waterway, and an accommodation bridge (long since demolished) erected to preserve his right of way. They rang the church bells all day when the canal reached Birmingham, and wild celebrations continued well into the night. The first section, completed in 1769, linked Birmingham with the mines at Wednesbury, and the price of coal is said to have halved. Interesting to reflect, then, that when the M40 motorway was extended from Oxford to the outskirts of Birmingham in 1990, no church bells rang with glee and no prices fell in the department stores of Corporation Street. During the rest of the 18th century, Birmingham became a magnet for canal promoters and, in 1794, the Birmingham Canal Navigations were formed, amounting to some 160 miles of waterway, of which 100 miles remain navigable in an area bounded by Wolverhampton, Walsall, Dudley and Tamworth.

There *were* celebrations, however, in 1991 when the Convention Centre opened alongside the canal, and Birmingham, here, has something to be proud of. Delegates from all over the world are wooed to convene in Birmingham instead of Brussels or Baltimore, and who knows what indelible magic of the BCN might rub off on them.

Brindley Place lies at the centre of things now. Here are 24 hour moorings overlooked by a plethora of cafe bars and restaurants - for once the hackneyed analogy of Birmingham with Venice seems almost understated, even disingenuous, and you cannot help but think that of all the British cities to see virtue in revitalizing their canals, Birmingham has made the best fist of it. From the piazzas of the Convention Centre the canal leads through Broad Street tunnel to Gas Street Basin, the epitome - and for many the lost soul - of Birmingham's waterways.

In fact Gas Street had come to symbolise the BCN to such an extent that it was often forgotten that the actual terminal wharf and offices of the Birmingham Canal lay to the east of here. Two arms terminated at the rear of the BCN company's handsomely symmetrical offices on Suffolk Street which, sadly, were demolished in 1928. Demolition

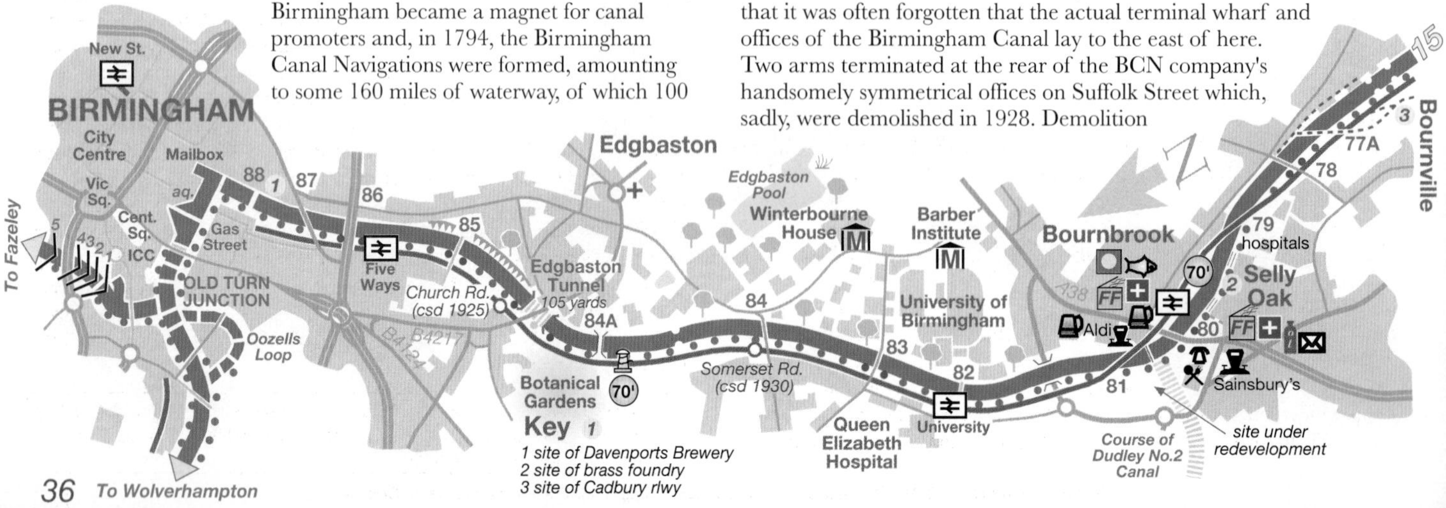

Key

1 site of Davenports Brewery
2 site of brass foundry
3 site of Cadbury rlwy

controversially took its toll of the Gas Street canalscape in 1975 as well, by which time the planners should have known better, and British Waterways were never really forgiven for razing their rich heritage of 18th century waterside warehouses to the ground in a calculated move to sidestep a preservation order.

For a time nothing was done to fill the void. Gas Street might have ceased to exist but for a community of residential boats which lent a splash of colour and humanity to a decaying canalscape. A decade elapsed before the developer's proposals were realised in bricks and mortar, and the biggest irony of all is that the new pubs and offices emerged in a warehouse vernacular style of remarkable similarity to the bulldozed originals. The only post Seventies interloper unsympathetic to the scale of the original Gas Street is the towering, shimmering, slippery, silvered edifice of the Hyatt Hotel. What do its sybaritic guests make of the little boats miles below their air-conditioned eyries? Do they see them as 'local colour', as archaic as the sampans of Hong Kong harbour?

The Worcester & Birmingham Canal

Work began on the Worcester & Birmingham Canal from the Birmingham end in 1794, but it was not until 1815 that the route was completed throughout. Fearful of its water supply disappearing down into the Severn, the Birmingham Canal Company at first refused to be directly linked with the newcomer, and so laborious transhipment of through traffic took place across an infamous divide known as the 'Worcester Bar'. Eventually, however, a stop lock was provided between the two waterways, affording the BCN some measure of protection, yet enabling through passage of boats.

Quickly extricating itself from the wine bars and nightclubs of downtown Birmingham, the Worcester & Birmingham Canal turns right-angle past The Mailbox development - together with its lofty neighbour, The Cube - and makes for the sylvan suburbs of Edgbaston. It was this cloistered, arboreous entrance to and exit from the city that prompted Robert Aickman to express the aphorism: "Canals stretch green fingers into towns." We can't help but share his enthusiasm, for this is a lovely stretch of canal - given its proximity to the city centre - and its towpath is increasingly used by walkers and cyclists as an alternative to the choked and inherently lethal carriageways of the A38.

In cahoots with the old Birmingham West Suburban Railway, opened in 1876, and now heavily nose to tail with suburban and inter-city trains, the canal skirts the purlieus of Birmingham University, whose Italianate tower 'Uncle Joe' stabs the sky. At Selly Oak there are plans - unrealised as yet - for part of the former Dudley No.2 Canal to be re-opened in conjunction with a retail development scheme led by Sainsbury's. Journeying southwards, the Worcester & Birmingham reaches the outskirts of the chocolate making centre of Bournville. Again there are scant remains of the canal's heyday, when its east bank was a busy point of interchange for Cadbury's fleet of narrowboats and its internal railway system shunted by its own fleet of perky tank locomotives painted in a dark red colour inspired by the company's cocoa tins.

Away2service's mobile 'service boat' operates in the vicinity of Old Turn Junction providing pump-out, fuel, gas, coal and repairs & servicing facilities. Tel: 0845 644 5344

15 WORCESTER & BIRMINGHAM CANAL King's Norton 4mls/0lks/1.5hrs

COMMERCIAL activity on the canal is sadly no longer considered a viable proposition, but leisure boating does bring its fair share of visitors to Cadbury World. Access from the offside visitor moorings is westwards along Bournville Lane which runs beneath the canal. Eastwards, you'll come upon two handsome rows of former shops labelled 'Bournville Markets' and Stirchley's imposing swimming baths, recently reborn (without the water) as a community hub.

Bournville's garden village owes its existence to the altruism of Quakers Richard and George Cadbury, who built a chocolate factory on a greenfield site in the vicinity in 1879. It was George in particular who had vision's of a worker's paradise, commissioning the architect Alexander Harvey to design artisans dwellings on a 120 acre site. Each house was to have a garden with fruit trees and a vegetable patch to provide an element of self-sufficiency - one cannot live on chocolate alone.

Between bridges 75 and 73 the towpath swaps sides, not on a whim, but because the Midland Railway once operated a transhipment basin on the west bank of the canal. At King's Norton the Stratford Canal comes in to join the Worcester & Birmingham, a route described on Maps 8 to 13. A sizeable paper mill formerly overlooked the canal junction and large quantities of coal were brought here by narrowboat from Black Country mines. The old Junction House is backed by the soaring steeple of St Nicholas, the parish church of King's Norton, where the Rev W. Awdry of *Thomas the Tank Engine* fame was a curate during the Second World War.

At 2,726 yards, Wast Hill Tunnel is the Worcester & Birmingham's longest. It takes around half an hour to pass through and, whilst appearances can be deceptive, rest assured that there *is* room to pass oncoming craft inside its gloomy depths. Like all Worcester & Birmingham tunnels (except Edgbaston), it has no towpath. The lads who led their boat

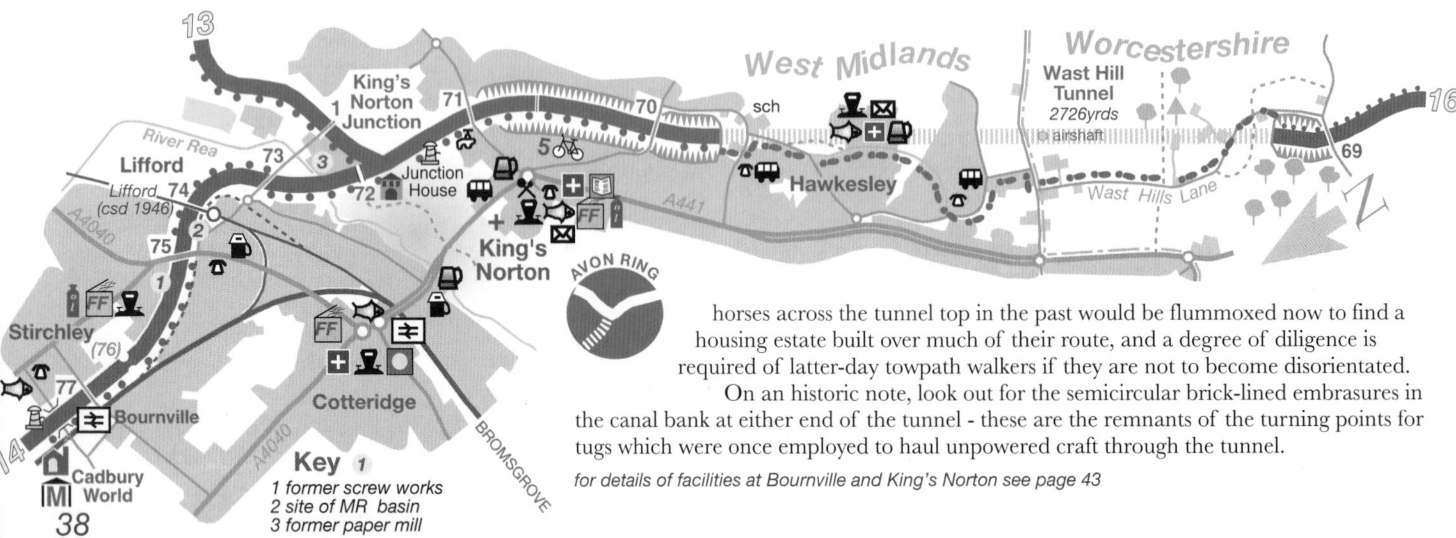

horses across the tunnel top in the past would be flummoxed now to find a housing estate built over much of their route, and a degree of diligence is required of latter-day towpath walkers if they are not to become disorientated.

On an historic note, look out for the semicircular brick-lined embrasures in the canal bank at either end of the tunnel - these are the remnants of the turning points for tugs which were once employed to haul unpowered craft through the tunnel.

for details of facilities at Bournville and King's Norton see page 43

16 WORCESTER & BIRMINGHAM CANAL Alvechurch 5mls/0lks/2hrs

POST-WAR Alvechurch overspills up its hillside to impinge upon the canal, but barely deflects from its dreamy, lock-less progress above the valley of the River Arrow. There are panoramic views eastwards towards Weatheroak Hill crossed by the Roman's Ryknild Street. A feeder comes in from Upper Bittell Reservoir beside an isolated canal employee's cottage near Bridge 66. The Lower Reservoir, rich in wildfowl, lies alongside the canal and is given a gorgeous wooded backdrop by the Lickey Hills. Only the Upper Reservoir feeds the canal, the Lower was provided to compensate millers whose water supplies from the Arrow had been detrimentally affected by construction of the canal. A short section of the canal was re-routed in 1985 to accommodate construction of the M42 motorway.

Bridge 62 carries the electrified commuter line from Redditch through Birmingham to Lichfield. A seventy-five minute train journey ... three days by boat to the nearest canal settlement at Fradley Junction. But time is an irrelevance on the canals, so relax and savour the charms of Shortwood Tunnel, its approach cuttings so suffocated by the odour of wild garlic that you feel as if you are being embraced by an over enthusiastic Frenchman. All that's missing is the tang of Gauloise, but then you may be able to provide that (and/or the Frenchman) yourself.

As with all other Worcester & Birmingham tunnels (Edgbaston excepted) the towpath isn't subterranean, but the old horse-path across the top remains well-defined, and it is pleasant to wander across the top, fantasising that you've a horse to lead while your boat is hauled through the earth beneath your feet by one of the erstwhile tunnel tugs as described so evocatively by Tom Foxon in his book *Number One*.

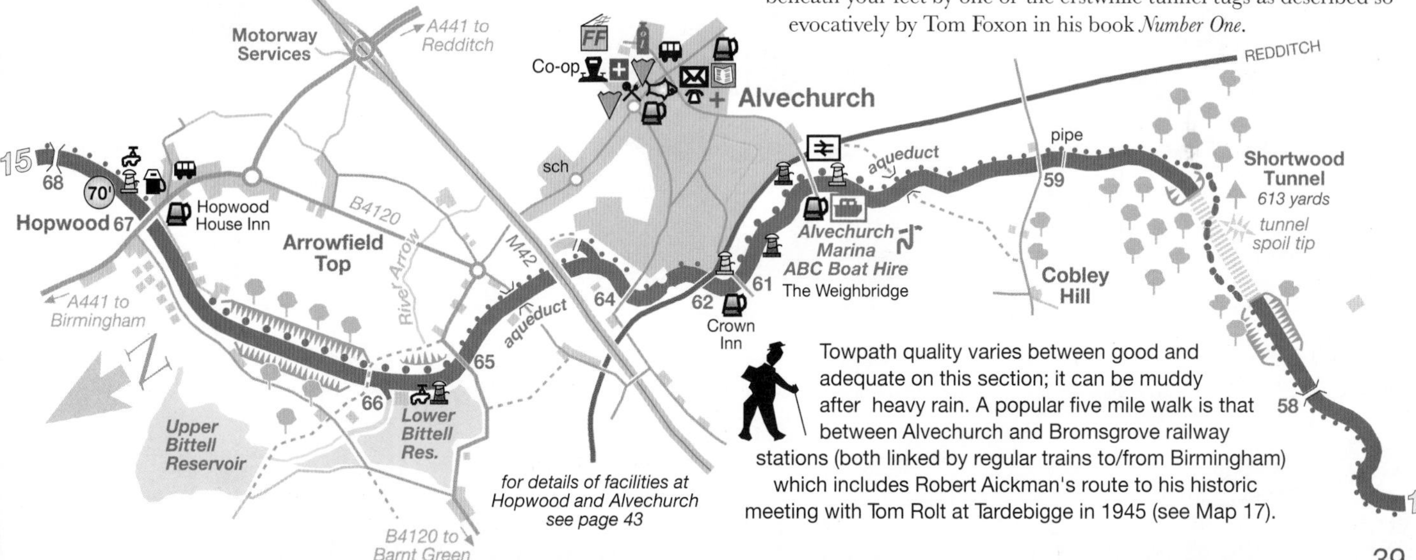

for details of facilities at Hopwood and Alvechurch see page 43

Towpath quality varies between good and adequate on this section; it can be muddy after heavy rain. A popular five mile walk is that between Alvechurch and Bromsgrove railway stations (both linked by regular trains to/from Birmingham) which includes Robert Aickman's route to his historic meeting with Tom Rolt at Tardebigge in 1945 (see Map 17).

Worcester & Birmingham

Tardebigge 1

Tardebigge 2

Tardebigge 3

Oddingley

Tardebigge 4

Sidbury Lock

Astwood 1

Robin Smithett

Astwood 2

Diglis

17 WORCESTER & BIRMINGHAM CANAL Tardebigge 4mls/36lks/7hrs

TARDEBIGGE represents a boater's Rite of Passage. Once you have tackled this flight which, coupled with the neighbouring six at Stoke, amount to thirty-six locks in four miles, other groups of locks, however fiendish, however formidable, pale into insignificance. The thirty chambers of the Tardebigge flight raise the canal over two hundred feet, the top lock - somewhat removed from the rest - being, at 14 feet, one of the deepest narrowbeam locks on the system; it replaced a lift dysfunctionally prone to recalcitrance and water wastage. Well maintained and surrounded by fine countryside, with wonderful views to the Malvern Hills, Tardebigge Locks are there to be enjoyed, not dreaded. And in the summer months you'll have plenty of fellow travellers with whom to share the experience, never mind the work. Tardebigge's 18th century church, with its slender 135ft spire, is an inspirational landmark: 'belatedly baroque' in the words of James Lees-Milne in his pithy 1964 *Shell Guide to Worcestershire*. Another spire to look out for - on the western horizon - is that of Bromsgrove's parish church, St John the Baptist.

Tardebigge holds a special place in the story of the inland waterways movement. It was to here that Robert Aickman and his wife made their way from Bromsgrove railway station to meet Tom and Angela Rolt aboard their narrowboat home *Cressy* which had been moored above the top lock throughout the Second World War. As a direct result of their meeting the Inland Waterways Association was formed. A plinth adjacent to the lock tells the story, along with a supplementary plaque correcting the date to 1945 - as Pearsons had immodestly and intuitively affirmed all along!

Only the briefest of pounds separates the Tardebigge and Stoke flights. Room enough, just, for half a dozen boats to moor for an overnight breather. The picturesque lock-keeper's cottage between locks 31 and 32 is available for holiday lets from the Landmark Trust, a body devoted to the rescue and refurbishment of worthwhile buildings in all shapes and sizes. A wheelbarrow is at the disposal of guests for the conveyance of luggage along the towpath. It was the demolition of the junction house at Hurleston, on the Shropshire Union Canal, which 'maddened' the Trust's founder, John Smith, into creating this laudable organisation in 1965.

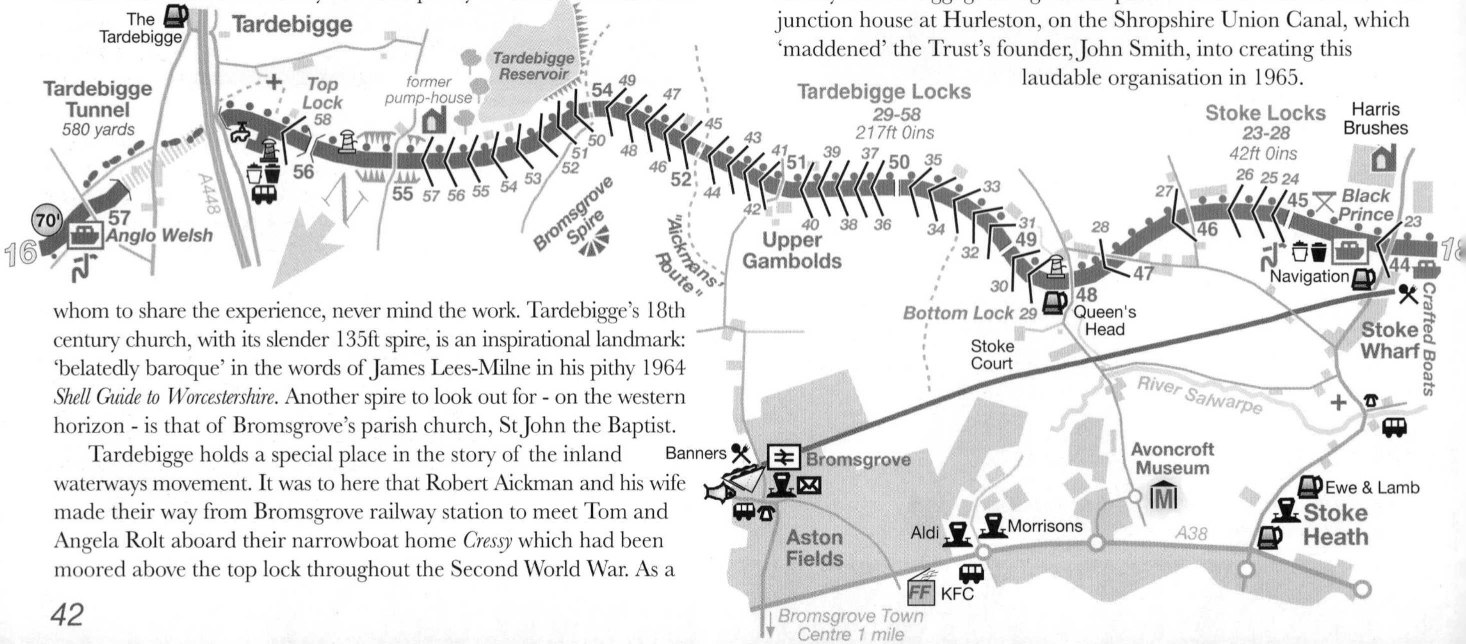

Bournville Map 15

Use of a CART 'facilities' key provides access from the secure offside moorings opposite Bournville railway station to the enchanting 'garden village' of Bournville and its arboreal street nomenclature.

Things to Do

CADBURY WORLD - Linden Road. Tel: 0844 880 7667. 'A whole world of chocolatey fun!' B30 2LU

SELLY MANOR - Maple Road. Tel: 0121 472 0199. Five minutes and five hundred years away from all that 'chocolatey fun'. B30 2AE

King's Norton Map 15

Arguably the most easily accessible facilities for canal travellers in this area. 48 hour moorings are provided between bridges 71 and 72 and it's only a short uphill walk to the centre, grouped about a pretty green and overlooked by the imposing spire of St Nicholas' Church. Queen Henrietta Maria stopped here overnight on her way to meet Charles I at Edge Hill. Half-timbered 17th century grammar school in churchyard.

Shopping

Facilities include: a pharmacy, Spar shop, post office, newsagent, off licence, and Lloyds bank.

Eating & Drinking

MOLLY'S - The Green. Tel: 0121 459 9500. Cheerful cafe, good for breakfasts. B38 8SD

Things to Do

ST NICHOLAS PLACE - Tel: 0121 458 1223. Heritage Centre adjoining church. Tours Fri & Sat. B38 8RU

Hopwood Map 16

HOPWOOD HOUSE INN - canalside Bridge 67. Tel: 0121 445 1716. Comfortably furnished Marston's 'Rotisserie' pub/restaurant open from noon. B48 7AB.

Petrol station with convenience store to south of Bridge 67. Small garden centre nearby. Buses to/from Birmingham.

Alvechurch Map 16

It's one thing strolling down from the canal, but an altogether different matter struggling back with shopping bags. Nevertheless, Alvechurch is a pleasant Worcestershire village with some worthwhile facilities.

Eating & Drinking

THE WEIGHBRIDGE - canalside Bridge 60. Tel: 0121 445 5111. The 'weighbridge house' for a coal wharf in days gone by. Tillerman's Tipple is brewed for them by Weatheroak. Home cooked food lunchtimes and evenings (ex Tue & Wed); breakfasts by prior arrangement. B48 7SQ

THE CROWN - canalside Bridge 61. Tel: 0121 445 2300. An unspoilt canalside pub. B48 7PN

There is also a Chinese takeaway (Tel: 0121 447 8085) and an Indian restaurant (Tel: 0121 445 5583).

Shopping

Co-op, post office (with newspapers) pharmacy, two butchers, off-licence, greengrocer and florist.

Connections

TRAINS - half-hourly service to Redditch and Birmingham. Tel: 03457 484950.

Aston Fields Map 17

Aston Fields, a suburb of Bromsgrove, has a number of shops - notably BANNERS deli and hot food outlet established as long ago as 1906 (Tel: 01527 872581 - B60 2DZ) and now they have opened an excellent cafe/restaurant as well (Tel: 01527 872889) open from 8am daily and providing evening meals Wed-Sat. Bromsgrove's railway station is here too, for taxis telephone Gold & Black on 01527 570707.

Stoke Wharf Map 17

A pair of stylishly refurbished pubs vie for your custom and offer just reward for the effort involved in working all those locks: QUEEN'S HEAD by Bridge 48 (Tel: 01527 557007 - B60 3AU) and the NAVIGATION by Bridge 44 (Tel: 01527 831600 - B60 4LB) where PRIORY CAFE (Tel: 01527 880660 - B60 4JZ) also provides eat in/take-away food Mon-Fri 6am-3pm, Sat 8am-12pm. AVONCROFT MUSEUM, a mile north of Bridge 48, houses a wonderful collection of buildings saved from demolition (Tel: 01527 831363 - B60 4JR).

Stoke Works Map 18

The BOAT & RAILWAY (Tel: 01527 831065 - B60 4EQ) is a Marston's/Banks's pub with a nice canalside terrace, good choice of beers and a wide range of bar meals (not Sundays) and a skittle alley. Take-away food is also available. The Worcester & Birmingham Canal Society regularly meet here.

Hanbury Wharf Map 18

At Hanbury Wharf the EAGLE & SUN (Tel: 01905 799266 - WR9 7DX) is a steak bar and carvery.

Dunhampstead Map 19

The quiet hamlet of Dunhampstead is able to offer both a canalside craft shop (Forge Crafts) and a well-appointed pub called THE FIR TREE INN (Tel: 01905 774094 - WR9 7JX) which serves tasty food and Hook Norton within its designer interior.

Tibberton Map 19

Many villages of this size can no longer muster a single pub, Tibberton manages two. The post office stores provide stamps, provender and gossip in equal measure, whilst postcards and prints by the local wildlife artist, John Horton, are on sale. Of the pubs, the BRIDGE INN (Tel: 01905 345874 - WR9 7NQ) is the more canal orientated, having a large waterside garden and offering a good choice of food; however the SPEED THE PLOUGH (Tel: 01905 345146 - WR9 7NQ) can equally be recommended. Buses connect the village with Worcester - Tel: 0871 200 2233.

18 WORCESTER & BIRMINGHAM CANAL Hanbury 4mls/6lks/2.5hrs

NOWADAYS, Britain's salt industry is largely confined to Cheshire but, as the name Droitwich suggests, this part of Worcestershire was once a centre of salt making too. The salt obsessed Romans built a special road between Droitwich and Alcester to carry this valuable commodity. Similarly, the Worcester & Birmingham built the short Droitwich Junction Canal from Hanbury Wharf to carry the same cargo. Abandoned in 1939, it has become one of the success stories of the canal restoration movement, finally re-opening in 2011 and forming, along with the Droitwich Barge Canal (see Map 21) what will undoubtedly become a hugely popular circular route - the Mid-Worcestershire Ring. If you're remaining loyal to the W& B's 'main line', it would be churlish not at least to stroll down the first three locks as far as Gateway Park, offering votive thanks as you go to those who steadfastly kept the faith with regard to the canal's second coming.

At the end of the 18th century, John Corbett, son of a local boatman, discovered large deposits of brine at Stoke Prior and developed one of the largest saltworks in the world on the site. It made his fortune. He met an Irish woman in Paris, married her and erected a replica French chateau for her on the outskirts of Droitwich, a town he transformed from one of industrial squalor into a fashionable spa. In its heyday the canalside works at Stoke was producing 200,000 tons of salt a year. The company had a fleet of fifty narrowboats and hundreds of railway wagons. Corbett died in 1901 and is buried at the pretty little church of St Michael's, Stoke Prior (Map 17). The 'John Corbett Way', a seven and a half mile waymarked trail, has been developed between Stoke Heath and Droitwich.

Attractive countryside returns at Astwood Locks, as canal and railway drift lazily through lush farmland overlooked by the wooded slopes of Summer Hill to the east. Westward views encompass Abberley and Woodbury hills beyond the River Severn. Closer at hand are the twin 700ft high masts of Wychbold radio transmitting station. Opened in 1934, its call sign "Droitwich Calling" became known throughout Britain and in many parts of Europe. During the Second World War Droitwich's long range transmitter broadcast the 'voice of freedom' throughout occupied Europe.

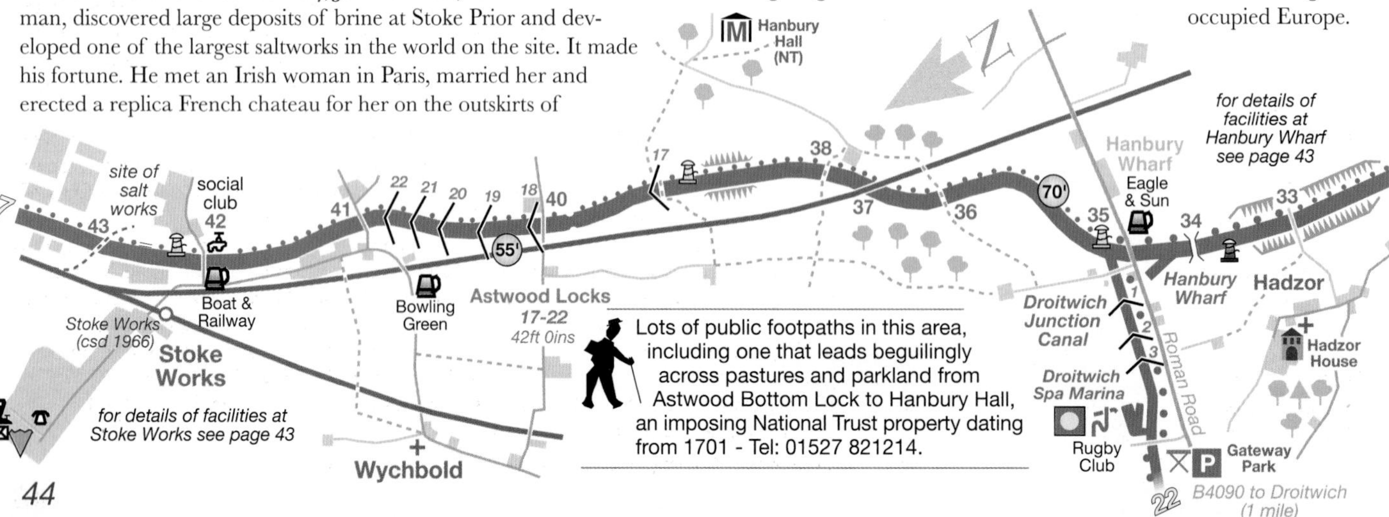

19 WORCESTER & BIRMINGHAM CANAL Oddingley 4mls/6lks/2hrs

THE canal skirts the mellow settlements of Shernal Green, Dunhampstead, Oddingley and Tibberton and, in spite of being sandwiched by the railway and motorway, seems remote and untouched. High clumps of sedge border the canal, swaying with the passage of each boat and somehow emphasising the loneliness of the landscape. At Shernal Green the Wychavon Way - a 42-mile long distance footpath running from Holt Fleet on the River Severn to Winchcombe in Gloucestershire - makes its way over the canal.

Dunhampstead Tunnel is tiny compared to the 'big three' to the north, but like them it has no towpath, forcing walkers to take to the old horse-path through deciduous woodlands above. A hire base adds traffic to the canal at this point, whilst a craft shop and convivial country pub provide an excuse to break your journey.

Oddingley consists of little more than an ancient manor house, a tiny church and a level-crossing keeper's cabin of typical Midland Railway style. Murder was done here in 1806! Visit the Fir Tree Inn for further details.

Tibberton is a long straggling village of mostly modern housing. Well-piled visitor moorings are provided west of Bridge 25.

A deep cutting and the M5 motorway separate Tibberton from Offerton Locks. Boating northwards you can now take a breather. Southbound the locks begin again as the Worcester & Birmingham completes its descent to the Severn. Worcester's industrial fringe makes its presence felt and muddy rugby players stomp across the footbridge at the tail of Lock 11. Worcester RUFC's impressive Sixways Stadium stands to the south of the canal. In an era where aggressive sobriquets are *de rigueur*, the Warriors are amongst the leading clubs in the country, but we like to think of the club's more gentlemanly origins in the 1870s when they played in 'white shirts and blue knickerbockers'. Hindlip Hall (4934 to fans of the old GWR), headquarters of the County Constabulary and refuge, in its original Elizabethan guise, of two members of the Gunpowder Plot, dominates the hillside to the north-west.

Two aspects of this canal's working practice were remarkable. Boats kept *left* when passing each other and pairs of donkeys were widely used in place of horses to haul the boats. The animals worked well together as long as they 'knew' one another, but the introduction of a new donkey would cause considerable ructions. One of the last traders on the Worcester & Birmingham Canal was Charles Ballinger of Gloucester. He was still using horse-drawn boats as late as 1954, carrying coal from the Cannock area to Townsend's mill at Diglis. Occasionally he would have an 'uphill' cargo as well: matches from Gloucester to Birmingham, or flour from Worcester to Tipton; but by the beginning of the Sixties trade had deserted the canal.

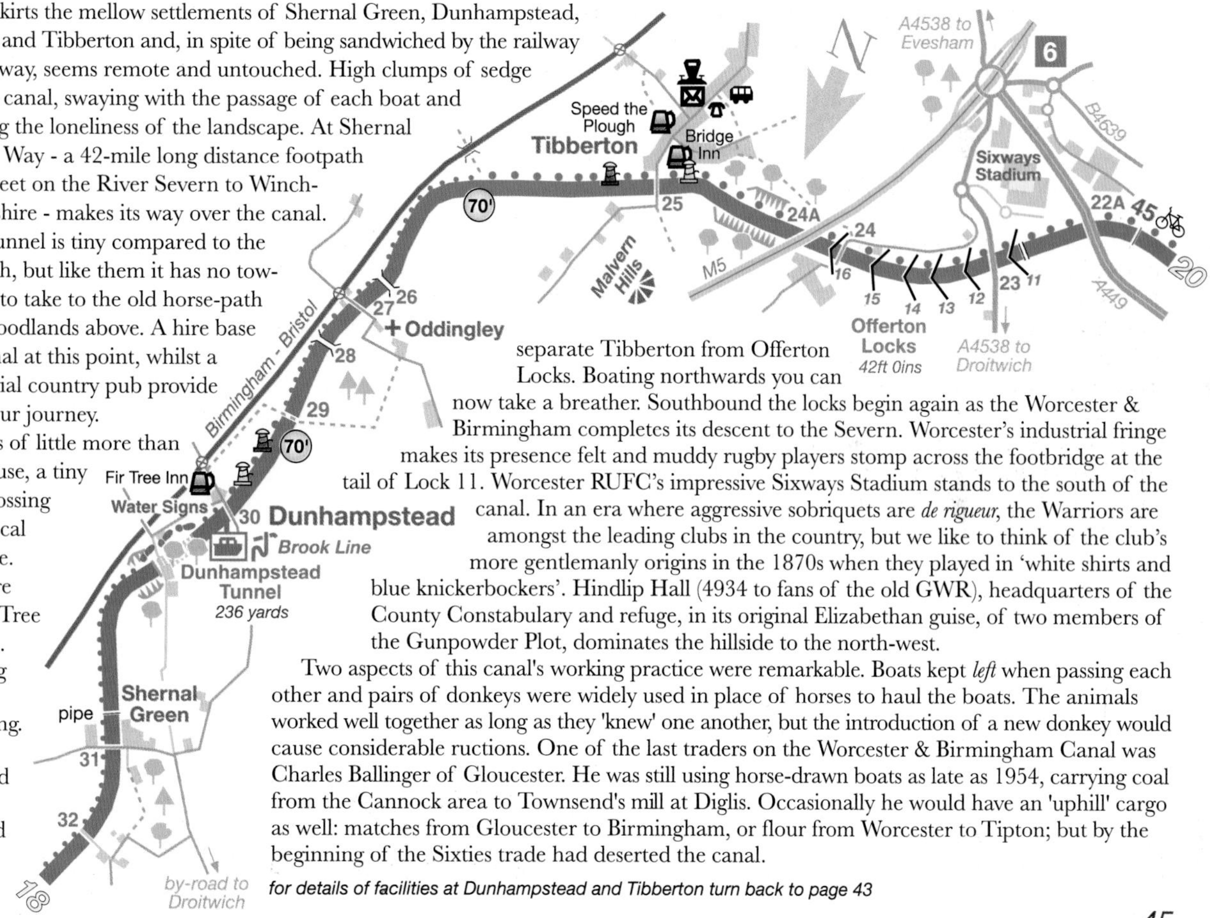

for details of facilities at Dunhampstead and Tibberton turn back to page 43

20 W & B CANAL, R. SEVERN Worcester 6mls/11lks/4hrs

WATERSIDE Worcester has always enjoyed a flagrant love affair with the Severn, but in modern times the canal has come into its own. From Tolladine down, the towpath is popular with pedestrians and cyclists alike. Burgeoning industrial estates accompany the canal but do little to spoil it. Cadbury's once had a busy wharf at Black Pole linked by water transport to their premises at Bournville and Frampton-on-Severn. A leisure centre and municipal golf course border the canal above Bilford Upper Lock. Worcester City sold their St George's Lane ground by Bridge 12 to property developers in 2013, and, after a period of playing their home games in Kidderminster have moved to Bromsgrove. North of Bridge 11 school playing fields are overlooked by an imposing pavilion.

A shapely railway bridge (10) spans the canal by Lowesmoor Wharf. It has a hole cut out of it, presumably to lessen the weight of the structure. Lowesmoor Wharf (aka Worcester Marina) is a good spot to moor securely close to the city centre - just slip beneath the roving bridge and ask permission at the office.

An Italianate clock tower peeps over the canal by Bridge 8, the former Engine Works of 1864. Known now as Shrub Hill Industrial Estate, within the confines of a corrugated-iron clad workshop, someone appears to be still archaically bashing-metal. In marked contrast, the premises of Pizza Hut overlook Bridge 5A. Locks at Blockhouse and Sidbury lower the canal towards the Severn. Between them, on the offside, Fownes Hotel was formerly a glove factory. Virtually opposite

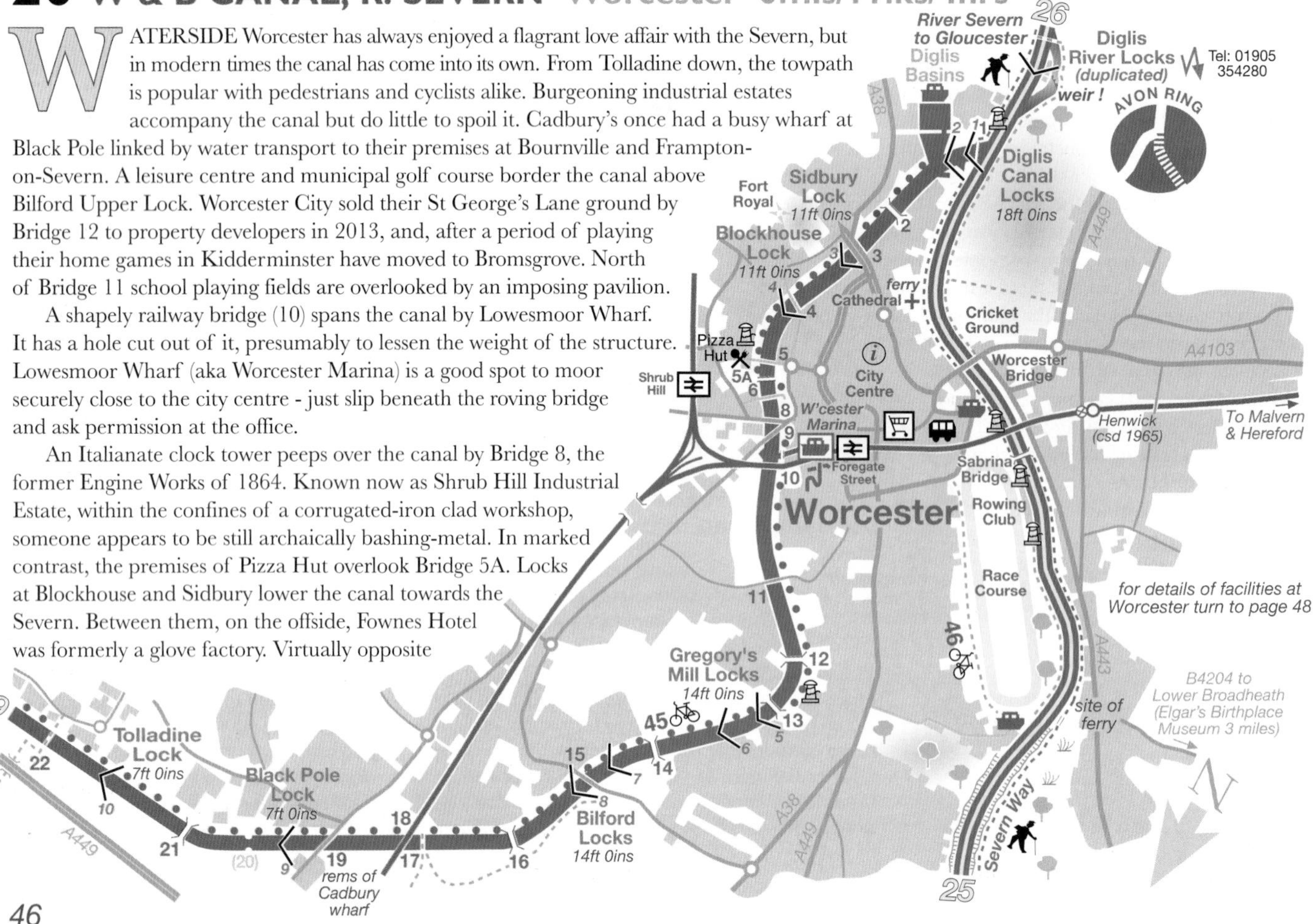

stands The Commandery, Charles II's headquarters during the Civil War Battle of Worcester in 1651, though it was originally a hospital and dates from as early as the 15th century. There is space here for some half a dozen boats to moor overnight within euphonious earshot of the cathedral clock. Sidbury Lock lies near the site of a gate in the city wall where a thousand Royalist troops are said to have been killed. Cromwell's men had captured the nearby fort and turned its canons on the escaping Cavaliers. The elevated fort is a pleasant park now, easily reached from the Commandery moorings. A panoramic plaque identifies major incidents of the Battle of Worcester and the gardens offer a marvellous view over the city. Bridge 3 carries amusing sculptures of Civil War pikestaffs, shields and helmets.

Burgeoning apartment blocks usher the canal down to Diglis. Townsend's Mill (by Bridge 2) once an intensive user of water transport, has been incorporated in these developments. Royal Worcester's porcelain works has not been so fortunate, and is gradually being redeveloped. Nowadays, what's left of the ceramic 'brand' is manufactured in either Stoke-on-Trent or Bangladesh!

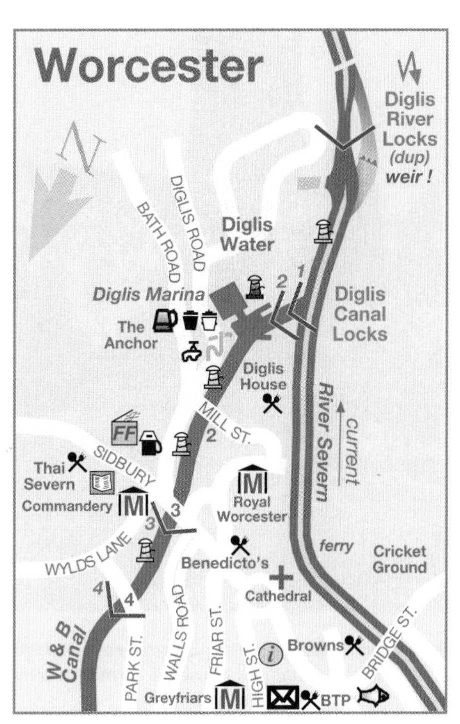

Diglis Basins opened in the 19th century to facilitate transhipment of cargoes between river and canal. One would have relished being here in their working heyday. Rebranded now as Diglis Water, they offer - to the amazement and incomprehension, one imagines, of the spirits of boatmen and dock workers who presumably haunt the place - 'a whole new environment for living and working in the modern world'.

Two broad locks separate the basins from the river. They are closed overnight, re-opening at eight in the morning. Entering or leaving the river can pose problems, especially if the current is flowing quickly, and getting your crew on or off for the locks needs careful consideration. One of the easiest access points is the pontoon immediately downstream of the lock entrance.

Downstream the river heads for Tewkesbury and Gloucester through Diglis River Locks. Upstream, 'Sabrina' flows beneath the great west window of the Cathedral, the juxtaposition of the noble building and the wide river being one of the great inland waterway scenes. A recent addition is King's School's striking, prow-shaped boathouse. On summer weekends a ferry operates in the vicinity of the Cathedral, and trip boats ply this reach as well, so keep a weather eye open for sudden manoeuvres.

Antiquated wharves and warehouses line the east bank of the river south of Worcester Bridge. Widened in the 1930s, the old parapet found its way into Edward Elgar's garden, so enamoured was the composer of anything associated with his home town. Limited official moorings are available on the city side between the old road bridge and the ornate, cast iron railway bridge which carries the pretty Malvern and Hereford line across the river. A third bridge spanning the Severn is of modern origin, being a stylish pedestrian link (much used by students) between the city centre and thewest bank suburbs: the Severn Way swaps sides at this point. Passingrowing clubs, the racecourse, and some enviable riverside properties -some of which would not look out of place beside the Thames - the rivertraveller heads upstream for more rural locales.

Worcester

Map 20

Descending from Birmingham to Worcester, the West Midlands are left intuitively behind, and you find yourself in streets where the patois has a distinct West Country burr - when it's not eastern European, that is. 'Royal' Worcester suffered more than most at the hands of the developers during the philistine Sixties (Ian Nairn, the late architectural writer and broadcaster, was incensed, and James Lees-Milne got into hot water for permitting his *Shell Guide to Worcestershire* to be too critical) but much making of amends has been done in recent years to enhance the city's fabric. The Cathedral, gazing devoutly over the Severn and containing the tomb of King John shares, with Gloucester and Hereford, Europe's oldest music festival, 'The Three Choirs'. From the deep well of Worcester's history you can draw inspiration from almost any era that captures your imagination. This was the 'faithful city' of the Civil War from which Charles II escaped following the final defeat of the Cavaliers. It was the home, for much of his life, of Sir Edward Elgar. Home too of that ensign of the empire, Lea & Perrins sauce; though they have recently lost their independence to Heinz. And here you'll find one of the country's loveliest cricketing venues, Worcestershire's New Road ground.

Eating & Drinking

THE ANCHOR - Diglis. Tel: 01905 351094. Marston's local alongside Diglis Basins. Breakfasts from 9.30am. Skittle alley and canalside patio. WR5 3BW

BENEDICTO'S - Sidbury. Tel: 01905 21444. Italian on the Cathedral side of Sidbury Lock. WR1 2HZ

BOSTON TEA PARTY - Broad Street. Tel: 01905 26472. Part of a growing chain (Barnstaple, Bath, Bristol, Birmingham etc) this charming cafe opens daily 7.30am (9am Suns) and offers a wide range of food and drinks all carefully (and mostly locally) sourced. WR1 3NF

Worcester Cathedral

Robin Smithett

BROWNS AT THE QUAY - Quay Street. Tel: 01905 21800. Stylish restaurant housed in former riverside mill (closed Mons). WR1 2JN

DIGLIS HOUSE HOTEL - Riverside. Tel: 01905 353518. Best to moor in basins and walk back for good bar and restaurant meals; nice views over the Severn towards the cricket ground. WR1 2NF

THAI ON 7EVERN - Sidbury. Tel: 01905 769054. Thai restaurant handy for moorings either side of Bridge 3 - turn left on reaching pavement. WR1 2HU

Shopping

The Shambles, Friar Street and New Street feature numerous fascinating little shops and small businesses. Crown Gate is the main shopping precinct with adjoining street markets on Tue-Sat. A new Asda supermarket in the St Martin's Quarter on Lowesmoor is easily accessible from bridges 8/9 and/or Worcester Marina. Also handy on Lowesmoor are convenience stores, a butcher, launderette and fish & chips.

Things to Do

TOURIST INFORMATION CENTRE - The Guildhall, High Street. Tel: 01905 726311. WR1 2EY

THE COMMANDERY - canalside by Sidbury Lock. Tel: 01905 361821. Civil War history museum. WR1 2HU

CITY MUSEUM & ART GALLERY - Foregate Street. Tel: 01902 25371. Admission free. One or two works by Benjamin Williams Leader (brother of the canal engineer Edward Leader Williams) perhaps best known for February Fill Dyke which hangs in Birmingham Art Gallery if you're going that way. WR1 1DT

TUDOR HOUSE - Friar Street. Tel: 01905 612309. Local history displays in five hunded year old half-timbered house. Admission free. WR1 2NA

MUSEUM OF ROYAL WORCESTER - Severn Street. Tel: 01905 21247. Sadly, all that's left of the famous pottery, though items still for sale. WR1 2ND

Connections

TRAINS - stations at Foregate Street and Shrub Hill. Services to/from the Malverns (and on through the hopyards to Hereford) Droitwich, Kidderminster, Birmingham etc. Good service also to and from London Paddington via Oxford and the picturesque Cotswolds line. Tel: 03457 484950.

BUSES - links throughout the area, but Diamond services 294/5 which connect Worcester with Stourport every couple of hours Mon-Sat, facilitate walks northwards along the Severn Way. First services 363/373 operate hourly Mon-Sat to Tewkesbury via Upton thus aiding southbound walks. Tel: 0871 200 2233. TAXIS - Cathedral Cars. Tel: 01905 767400.

Droitwich Canals

Hotel boats near Mildenham

21 DROITWICH CANALS Hawford & Salwarpe 4mls/8lks/4hrs*

‘THERE are no wide prospects or startling beauties along this Salwarpe valley; it is for those who appreciate the smaller things - the noble trees on the slopes, the rich green of the meadows on the valley floor, still waters, and the quiet of deep country.’ That was how Tom Rolt described the course of the Droitwich Barge Canal in 1949, by which time it had already been officially abandoned for a decade. Or should that be ‘by *wych* time’? ... for wych was the name given to the smaller trows specially built to navigate from Droitwich down to the Severn with cargoes of salt, and Rolt, like us, was the sort of man who would have relished seeing such vessels going about the work for wych they had evolved.

Officially abandoned in 1939 - though disused as far as the Barge Canal was concerned by 1916, and 1929 in the case of the Junction - largely unused since the First World War, the seven and a bit miles of waterway between Hawford on the Severn and Hanbury on the Worcester & Birmingham Canal had decayed to such an extent that anyone with an ounce of common sense would have known that they were beyond redemption. Fortunately, canal enthusiasts are not noted for their common sense. As David Hutchings once put it, in a tongue in cheek reference to restoration of the Stratford Canal: ‘we were none of us experts, otherwise we’d have known it couldn’t be done’. When one sailed past the entrance lock at Hawford, buried in someone’s front garden, and thought of how the A449’s embanked dual-carriageway had been callously laid across the line of the canal, restoration seemed implausible. In the final analysis, the canals’ shortness excited potential as opposed to consigning them to irrelevance. That and the fact that they were connected at either end with flourishing waterways which, taken as a whole, could be effectively trumpeted as a ‘mini-ring’ *par excellence.* In short, the scene was set for a revival: British Waterways’ final flourish before being transformed from a nationalised industry into a charitable organisation.

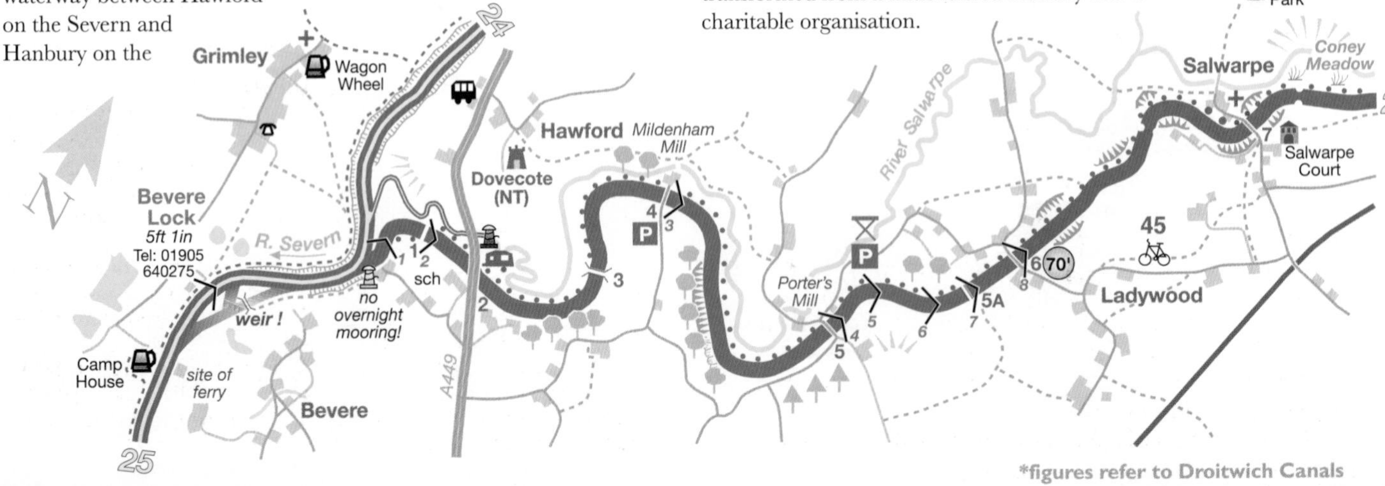

*figures refer to Droitwich Canals

Eight (not too onerous) broad-beam locks carry the Barge Canal (surveyed by James Brindley but engineered by John Priddey and opened in 1771) up from the Severn at Hawford to its summit pound at Ladywood. Not to put too fine a point on it, the scenery is spell-binding. An audio trail (downloadable from Waterscape) has been recorded to interpret the canal's progress. Quite frankly, though, the soundtrack provided by nature is what you should really be listening to: cuckoos, chiff-chaffs, reed warblers; the murmur of insects, the munching of cattle; the inculcating breeze in the reed beds. At times the reeds are so high and thick that the canal and the towpath seem like separate entities, not yet introduced to each other.

Hawford Duckweed

Above Lock 2 the canal borders the grounds of a prep school before plunging into a newly-provided concrete tunnel beneath the A449. It doesn't take long, however, for the noise of traffic to be left behind, balm being provided by swaying poplars; some bearing mistletoe, should you need an excuse to kiss your companion*. The bridges carry attractive blue number plates which have a sort of French feel about them. No.3 is also known as Linacre Bridge and it is one of the canal's original occupation bridges. Bridge 4, Mildenham Bridge, abuts Lock 3 and nearby is a retired example of several mills which were once a feature of the river valley. Looking at the Salwarpe today, it's difficult to imagine there ever being enough flow in it to power machinery.

A shallow cutting carries the canal away from the top lock and presently views open out across charmingly unspoilt countryside. The channel narrows at the site of a former swing-bridge. The cuttings at Salwarpe are much deeper and more bosky, whilst the canal bends sharply to pass beneath the high arch of Bridge 7. Cyclists are asked to dismount and boaters recommended to toot their horns to avoid an embarrassing meeting of bows on the bend. Sequestered at the end of a No Through Road, Salwarpe is notable for two fine buildings: St Michael's Church (with its giant Thuja trees, grown from seeds brought back from Tanganyika) and Salwarpe Court, a substantial 16th century house of half-timber and herring-bone brick. The entrance to Coney Meadow nature reserve lies alongside another abandoned swing-bridge.

*The person with you, that is, not this guide book!

⚠ Advice for Boaters

1 Approaching the Droitwich Barge Canal from the Severn at Hawford you'll find two mooring pontoons. That on the left, nearest the lock itself, is for use when entering the lock. The one on the right is for waiting only and overnight mooring is prohibited.

2 To protect the privacy of the occupants of the cottage alongside Lock 4 access is restricted. Going uphill the person setting the lock will need to cross the road bridge to the offside. Going downhill a Watermate key will be required to reach the lockside.

3 River level gauges exist at Lock 1 on the Barge Canal, at Barge Lock in central Droitwich and at locks 6 and 7 on the Junction Canal.

4 Bridge 5 on the Junction Canal has restricted and variable headroom. Check for oncoming boats before proceeding.

22 DROITWICH CANALS Droitwich & Hanbury Wharf 3.5mls/8lks/3hrs

DROITWICH wears its suburbs lightly, indeed the canal curtails them, and the towpath side of the Barge Canal's entrance from the south is bordered by playing fields and public open spaces. As it reaches the centre of town - once a Dantesque scene of brine-extraction and evaporation - the canal passes beneath two railway bridges overlooked by a classic Great Western signal box and some fine examples of lower quadrant semaphore signals. Bridge 16 carries Kidderminster Road over the canal and ushers in Netherwich Basin where an inviting semi-circle of secure 'fishbone' moorings are available, both for permanently moored craft and visitors.

Vines Park creates a delightful environment for the formal meeting of the Barge and Junction canals at Barge Lock. It derives its name from the Roman's vinicultural activities in the area.

Where at the height of the town's industrial past the canalside would have thronged in a steamy, smokey haze of salt works and brine pits, now it's a green sward, a public amenity enhanced by the return of boats and all the colourful activity they engender. Interestingly, the original line of the canal lies under the Saltway, but there is a cohesive quality about the new line which makes it appear entirely plausible. A re-creation of the wych trow *Volunteer* reminds all and sundry of why the Barge Canal was built in the first place, and the statue of Saint Richard confirms that at least two miracles have occurred in the vicinity.

A trio of swing-bridges add charm to the canal's passage through Vines Park - a quartet if you count the one which spans the Barge Lock itself. They are padlocked to deter hooliganism, and you will need your trusty CART facilities key to unlock them. Owing to subsidence brought about by brine extraction, Barge Lock is an astonishing fourteen feet higher than as originally built. The canal joins the river

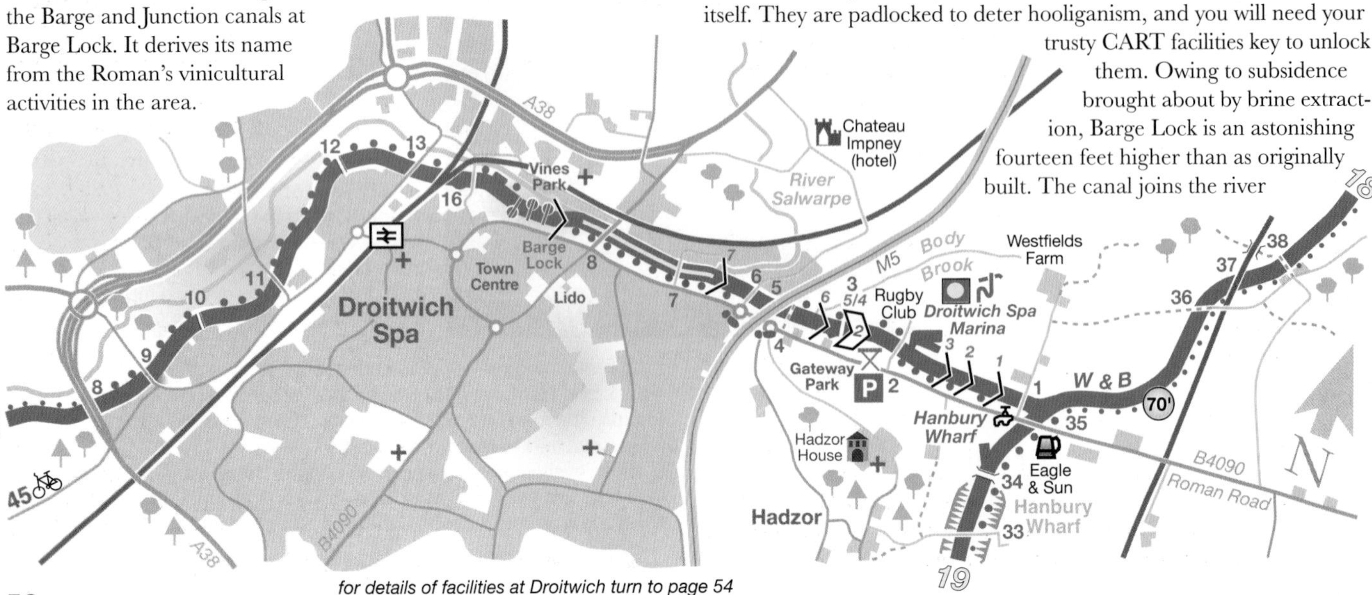

for details of facilities at Droitwich turn to page 54

at this point and, depending on fluctuations in water level, the lock may not require filling or emptying at all; though the gates should be closed after use. Under the watchful eye of St Augustine's church (its tower blackened by wafting smoke from the salt works), the navigation passes beneath another Bridge 8, the Junction Canal's bridges being numbered downwards to Hanbury Wharf. Handsomely decked out in gold paint, some credulity needs stretching to picture the era when the bridge featured a chapel. What a shame it was demolished in the 18th century, otherwise Droitwich could have joined the exclusive company of Rotherham, Bradford-on-Avon, Wakefield and the Cambridgeshire St Ives in retaining their bridge chapels.

In returning navigability to the Droitwich Junction Canal (opened by the Worcester & Birmingham Canal Company a little matter of seventy-three years after the Barge Canal) it has been necessary to detour from the original route to/from the town centre, resulting in a longer length of the River Salwarpe being adopted. Evidence of the former route of the canal can be seen in the form of an abandoned arch on the towpath side just east of Bridge 8. The Salwarpe is now utilised as far as Lock 7 - a different lock 7, you'll appreciate, from the Barge Canal's Lock 7 near Ladywood on Map 21. This Lock 7, moreover, is completely new, and functionally built from concrete without the wing walls which traditionally nudge steerers into lock chambers; hence, perhaps, the requirement for two large blue and white, motorway-like arrows to be displayed indicating exactly where the 'hole' you should head for is!

It is fortunate that a culvert, provided to pass Body Brook beneath the M5 motorway, is of sufficient dimensions for narrowboats to squeeze through, otherwise the cost - let alone upheaval - of constructing a tunnel to carry the new line of the canal beneath the motorway might have rendered the whole project untenable. As things are, it's a tight enough squeeze, and even the gentle flow of Body Brook can make gaining headway a slow process travelling uphill. Lay-bys are provided at either end of what is known as Bridge 5 to hold back should an oncoming boat have already begun to pass beneath the motorway.

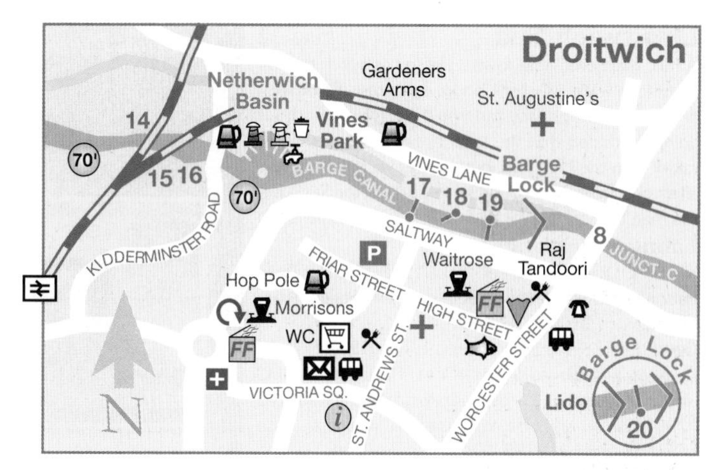

It will have already become apparent that the Junction Canal exudes an entirely different atmosphere to the Barge Canal, and not merely that it's narrower. Views along it are much more open and it attracts an altogether different class of flora and fauna. Raw as yet, it has the look of a freshly dug garden pond. Three brand new locks - two of them merged into a 'staircase' pair with shared centre gates - lift the canal up past the gentlemanly (and gentle*womanly*) 'thugs' of Droitwich Rugby Club, again on a slightly different alignment to the original. A car park and picnic site encourage exploration of the new canal, whilst above Bridge 2 a two-hundred berth marina has been constructed, probably very necessarily; this is likely to prove an extremely popular canal.

Regaining its original course, the canal ascends through three very deep (and original) locks equipped with operating side ponds to join the Worcester & Birmingham Canal at Hanbury Wharf. Small but incredibly beautiful, the revitalised Droitwich Canals seem like £12m well spent, even if you simply go by the look of happiness on the faces of the people using it, whatever their means of propulsion.

Droitwich Spa Map 22

A mild-mannered little town - pleased as punch to have a working waterway back on its doorstep - Droitwich revels in its salty past and you'll not go far without being reminded that the local brine is thirteen times saltier than the Med. Two local heroes vie for the town's affections: Saint Richard and John Corbett, the Salt King, the man responsible for the town's jaunty appellation

Eating & Drinking

HOP POLE - Friar Street. Tel: 01905 770155. *Good Beer Guide* listed town pub easily reached from Netherwich Basin. WR9 8ED

GARDENERS ARMS - Vines Lane. Tel: 01905 772936. Congenial pub adjacent Vines Park. WR9 8LU

SPINNING WHEEL - St Andrews Street. Tel: 01905 770031. Friendly cafe/restaurant & wine bar with courtyard garden. WR9 8DY

RAJ TANDOORI - Worcester Street. Tel: 01905 770051. Indian restaurant housed somewhat incongruously in half-timbered town house. WR9 8LA

Shopping

Waitrose's supermarket couldn't be handier, and Morrisons (with its recycling point) isn't far from the canal either. Independent shops (such as Lymers Butchers) along the subsidence-wrought High Street. Chain stores in St Andrews Precinct with its award-winning loos.

Things to Do

TOURIST INFORMATION & HERITAGE CENTRE - Victoria Square. Tel: 01905 774312. WR9 8DS

LIDO - Lido Park. Tel: 01905 799342. Outdoor saltwater heated swimming! WR9 8AA

Connections

TRAINS - London Midland services to/from Worcester, Birmingham, Kidderminster etc. Tel: 03457 484950

TAXIS - NY Taxis. Tel: 01905 776414.

Junction Canal Bridge 6

Bridge 5

Leaving Droitwich

Junction Canal Lock 3

Cliffey Wood

River Severn

23 RIVER SEVERN Stourport-on-Severn 4mls/1lk/1hr

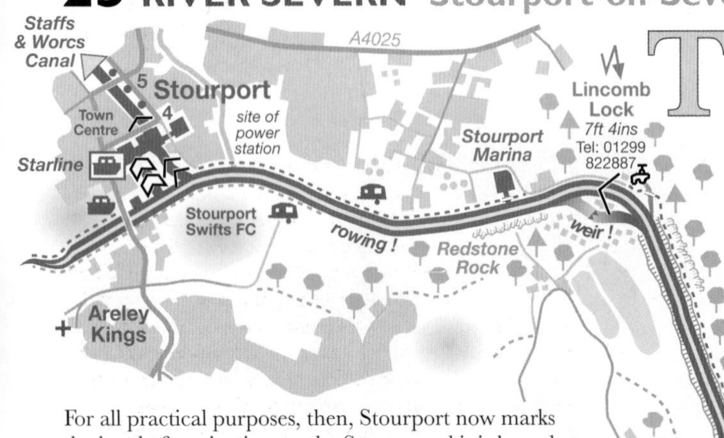

THERE was a Wordsworthian time when the Severn could be navigated commercially all the way upstream to the outskirts of Welshpool: Pool Quay - see Map 35 *Welsh Waters*. We boaters can only daydream of such voyages now: up through the Ironbridge Gorge, cradle of the industrial revolution; past the site of the Roman settlement of Uriconium; all but boxing the compass at Shrewsbury, islanded by a Housmanesque Severn stream. But such facilities, alas, were progressively abandoned during the second half of the 19th Century, as the railways robbed the river of its trade. The railways in turn became viewed as obsolete. We have a propensity - as a race? ... as a species? - to anti-poetically undo great works. Up until 1963 you could catch a direct train from Stourport to Shrewsbury. Now the traveller between those two points has no recourse but to go by road. Progress, perhaps, is a dish that has been too long in the oven. In recent years there have been campaigns to restore navigation - which theoretically remains a 'right' - at least as far as Shrewsbury. But, as with the majority of such well-meaning schemes, finance rather than engineering is the inhibiting factor, the fly in the ointment. Should you wish to venture a bit further, avail yourselves of one of the little motor launches by Stourport Bridge and go put-putting upstream.

For all practical purposes, then, Stourport now marks the head of navigation on the Severn, and it is here that the through traveller by water exchanges the fluctuating currents of the river for the stolid waters of the Staffordshire & Worcestershire Canal.

Stourport itself suffers from a personality disorder: half convinced that it's a seaside town; half a rich heritage of canal wharves. But whether you have come here for a ninety-nine and a knees-up, or to pay more serious homage to Brindley's basins, Stourport rarely disappoints. To moor in the Upper Basin, listening to time being measured by the quarter beats of the clocktower's sonorous bell, is one of the inland waterways' most magical experiences. And whatever entrance the boater makes - locking up from the Severn under the benign gaze of the Tontine Hotel, or descending into the dripping depths of York Street Lock from the canal - there will be few steerers able to resist exploration of the basins, shunting back and forth like some busy tug; turning in wide arcs or honing their reversing skills. The original and largest - known as the Upper Basin - opened in 1771, and connects through two wide-beam 'barge' locks with the river. These impressive (at least in narrowboater's eyes) chambers were built sturdily enough to withstand the Severn's perennial propensity for flooding, and capacious enough for the indigenous Severn Trows. Between the barge locks lies the smallest basin, thought to have been used as an assembly point and not as a wharf as such. A second link to the river, consisting of four narrow-beam locks in pairs of staircases, was opened in 1781. Here again the locks are separated by a small basin from which a drydock extends. Manoeuvring a lengthy boat between the staircase pairs can be tricky, and it doesn't help one's sangfroid that there is often a sizeable crowd of onlookers who will gain as much entertainment from your technique as from the adjacent fairground. At the top of the narrow locks, and contemporary with their construction, lies the Clock Basin, interconnected with the Upper Basin. On a peninsula between these upper, boat-filled expanses of water stands the glorious Clock Warehouse, headquarters these days of the Stourport Yacht Club whose vessels migrate up-river to winter in the security of the basins.

Once there were two basins which lay to the east of Mart Lane. Known expediently as the 'Further-most Basins', they dated from the early 19th century. The lower, reached through a wide lock, had a brief existence, closing in 1866 when the town gas works took over the site. The other basin flourished in an Indian Summer of commercial activity between 1926 and 1949 when coal boats for the power station discharged in it; their dusty black cargoes of Cannock coalfield slack being unloaded by electric grab and carried in hoppers along an aerial ropeway to the power station's furnaces. Subsequently it was infilled and a timber yard occupied its site, but it has been re-excavated as a major focal point of the regeneration scheme and is jostled now by modern apartments.

Another important element of the redevelopment of Stourport Basins concerns the return to life of the Tontine Hotel, refurbished for use as housing, but at the time of our most recent visit still unoccupied. It derived its unusual name from a system of speculative life insurance, the last surviving member of its original group of investors gaining full ownership of the building: fuel for skulduggery one imagines and the possibility of a plot which would inspire most detective story writers. In its heyday it boasted a hundred bedrooms, a ballroom and formal gardens spilling down to the riverbank.

The 'narrow boat' route through the basins at Stourport - from river to canal and vice versa - involves negotiating two staircase locks which are unusual in that there is no need to ensure that the lower chamber is empty when going down as overflow weirs automatically equate the levels. When joining the river and heading downstream, it's not a bad idea to telephone ahead to Lincomb Lock to let the keeper know you're coming.

The River

The Severn's official head of navigation is just upstream of Stourport Bridge where the Gladder Brook enters from the west bank, though occasional convoys of shallow-draughted diehards do journey upstream to Bewdley campaigning to restore navigation to the Upper Severn. One waterway project which did not materialise was for a canal from Stourport to Leominster. A token sod was dug opposite the basins in 1797, but the ludicrously ambitious through route never came to fruition. Stourport Bridge - the fourth on the site - was erected in 1870 to the designs of one Edward Wilson, an engineer involved in the construction of railways in the district at the time. It is notable for its unusual spiral staircase.

The River Stour's confluence with the Severn is muted, and no trace remains of Stourport's grandiose riverside power station, opened with a flourish by Stanley Baldwin in 1926 and demolished in the Eighties. Caravans and camping accompany the river down to Redstone Rock, a refuge for outlaws in Cromwell's time. The wharves opposite, together with the industrial estate to the rear, were developed by the Severn & Canal Carrying Company in the nineteen-thirties. A considerable volume of oil traffic was dealt with here until the spread of pipelines in the Sixties. Stourport Marina reflects the Severn's present day emphasis on leisure, but it would be nice if Harker's and Regent Oil's petrol barges still plied the river.

Pending any progress with the Upper Severn scheme, Lincomb Lock is the highest on the Severn. It lies in a picturesque setting dominated by one of the sheer red sandstone cliffs which characterise the river in this part of the world. Downstream, on the port side, there is evidence of a petroleum jetty and camouflaged oil dumps dating back to the Second World War. Further on, the frivolities of Stourport-on-Sea are rapidly forgotten as the Severn - apparelled, perhaps, in celestial light and

continued overleaf:

continued from page 57:
vouchsafed intimations of its own immortality - glides through some delightful Worcestershire countryside.

Pedestrians can enjoy the river by walking the Severn Way which keeps to the east bank between Stourport and Holt Fleet. Refreshment opportunities are, however, beyond reach since the ferries at Hampstall and Lenchford ceased to operate long ago. In 1919 the former was swamped in the wake of a passing steamer and sank, drowning nine unsuspecting unfortunates. Tragedy is never far from water.

It is difficult to grasp that Dick Brook, emerging imperceptibly from the woods on the west bank, was made navigable in the 17th Century to serve an iron forge located deep in the woods: woods which incidently are famous for their lime trees. L. T. C. Rolt moored here aboard *Cressy* and described the experience in topographical study *Worcestershire* published by Robert Hale in 1949. Gardening enthusiasts will recall that Clacks Farm played host to broadcasts of the BBC's *Gardeners World* for a number of years.

Stourport — Map 23

Water on the brain has left Stourport under the illusion that it's a coastal resort. All the trappings are here: funfairs and fish & chips, steamer trips, paddling pools and amusement arcades. Day trippers pour in from the West Midlands to let their hair down and make believe they are really in Rhyl or Barmouth. Marginally more in touch with reality, us boaters can swagger about the town pretending that we've just come up with a cargo of oil from Avonmouth.

Eating & Drinking

THE ANGEL - riverside. Tel: 01299 822661. Marston's/Banks's local on the riverbank. DY13 9EW

BLOSSOM'S - York Street. Tel: 01299 829442. Quaint canalside tea room. DY13 9EE

NAMASTE - Lichfield Street. Tel: 01299 877448. Indian restaurant adjacent Bridge 4. DY13 9EU

ROSMARIO - High Street. Tel: 01299 823900. Italian & Mediterranean cooking. DY13 8DH

THE WINDLASS - Stourport Basins. Tel: 01299 871742. Cafe/restaurant housed in former canal workshop and stable. DY13 9EW

Shopping

Co-op (with post office), Tesco Metro and Lidl supermarkets at the top end of town. Boots and W. H. Smith on the High Street. And whilst on High Street look out for Grinnall's excellent greengrocers,

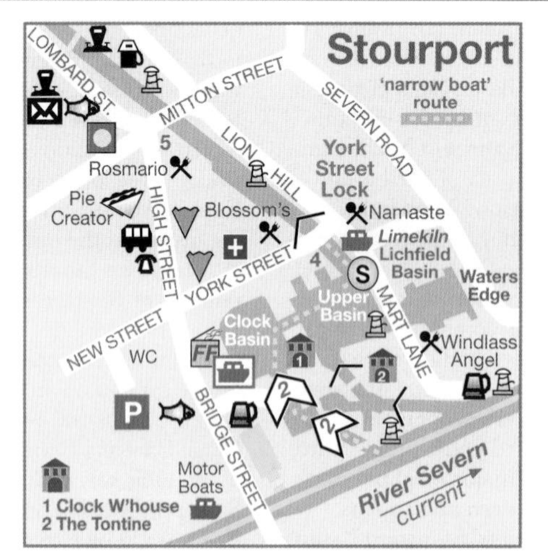

and the mouth-watering premises of The Pie Creator. Across the street, Gough's do gluten free pies.

Connections

BUSES - Diamond 3 and X3 link Stourport with Kidderminster every 10 minutes, Mon-Sat and hourly Sun. Diamond service 294/5 runs bi-hourly Mon-Sat to/from Worcester providing a useful service for Severn Way walkers. Tel: 0871 200 2233.

TAXIS - Pardoe's. Tel: 01299 824924.

Holt Fleet — Map 24

Good place to stop on the Severn, a pontoon being provided between the tail of the lock and the bridge.

Eating & Drinking

THE HOLT FLEET - west bank. Tel: 01905 620286. Architecturally ostentatious Thirties 'road house', now a family-owned inn/restaurant. Small jetty. WR6 6NL

THE WHARF INN - east bank. Tel: 01905 620337. Lengthy customer moorings. WR6 6NN

Other riverside pubs between Holt and Stourport include the LENCHFORD INN (Tel: 01905 620229 - WR6 6TB) and the HAMPSTALL INN (Tel: 01299 822600 - DY13 0RY); both offer customer moorings.

Shopping

Convenience store (gas, coal and logs) and recycling point. The apple growers, Broomfields, have a farm shop and tea room on the road up to Holt Heath.

Grimley — Map 24

WAGON WHEEL - Tel: 01905 640340. Charming thatched and whitewashed country pub. WR2 6LU

Bevere — Map 24

THE CAMP HOUSE - riverside downstream of Bevere Lock. Tel: 01905 640288. Peacocks in the garden, Bathams beer and rabbit pie render this isolated riverside inn a veritable heaven on earth. Limited moorings for customers. WR2 6LX

24 RIVER SEVERN Holt Fleet & Bevere 5mls/2lks/1.5hrs

HOW is Worcestershire? sang the Stourport-born singer /songwriter, Clifford T. Ward, and from these exceedingly pleasant reaches of the Severn you have little alternative other than to reply: still very lovely indeed. This is Britain's - rather than England's - lengthiest river: 221 miles in case you were wondering. It seems rather inadequate, that, at 42 miles, less than a fifth of it is currently navigable; a peculiarly British embarrassment. Neither is it legal to follow the whole of the Severn's course on foot - entrenched landowning interests have seen to that - and at Holt Fleet the Severn Way is forced into a lengthy, though not in itself uninteresting, detour.

Holt Lock is picturesquely sited beneath high cliffs somewhat reminiscent of Stoke Bardolph on the Trent. Downstream the river passes beneath an elegant iron bridge designed by Thomas Telford and dated 1827. Traffic over it is heavy and it has recently been in need of remedial work to - if you'll pardon two puns - *halt* the decay and further its *life* span. From the river there are views of Holt Castle, the pele tower dating from the 14th century.

It is no longer necessary for enthusiasts to speak melancholically of the Droitwich Barge Canal in the past tense. The re-opening of this long abandoned waterway is a remarkable achievement, as described in the text accompanying Maps 21 and 22. The last in the trio of automated locks which separate Stourport from Worcester is to be found at Bevere. Following restoration of the Droitwich canals, and the mini-ring thus formed, boat passages through the lock are likely to increase severalfold. Note Telford's charming little bridge which spans the weir stream.

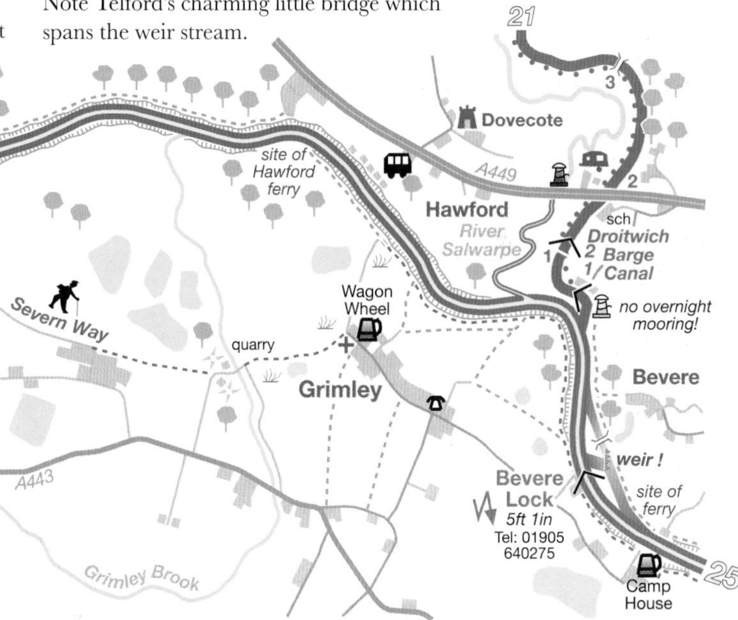

25 RIVER SEVERN Worcester 4mls/1lk/1hr

WORCESTER'S affection for its riverside is clear, though perhaps not quite so commercially exploited as in its Edwardian heyday. We're all a bit too well-travelled now to be as excited at the thought of a steamer trip or a jaunt in a rowing boat as our forebears used to be, but there is much to be said for such innocent pleasures, and it is good to see that the opportunity to indulge in such frivolities is still possible at Worcester. Old photographs expose a gallimaufry of vessels jostling for position: trows, tugs, lighters and narrowboats; paddle steamers, launches, rowing eights and skiffs. Once it must have seemed that the whole world and his wife wanted to be on the water.

Worcester's National Hunt race course can trace its riverside origins back as far as 1718. Then, as now, race meetings could be disrupted by the course finding itself under water. A recent revival has been the 'Land O'Plums' race which used to be run at Pershore up until around the time of the Second World War.

The railway bridge across the river is approached from Foregate Street station on a sinuous viaduct of 68 arches. Between this and Worcester Bridge stands the steamer quay and visitor moorings. Handsome warehouses overlook the river, as does the redundant spire of St Andrews, nicknamed the 'Glovers' Needle' on account of one of the city's former trades. Thankfully, the Cathedral is far from redundant, and, amongst many other treasures, contains the tomb of King John. A recent addition to the riverside scene is King's School's striking, prow-shaped boathouse.

Worcestershire County Cricket Club's New Road ground can lay legitimate claim to being one of the most beautiful in the world. Seeking a suitable location to play, the club rented three 'sheep fields' from the Dean and Chapter of Worcester Cathedral. The first county match was against Yorkshire at the commencement of the 1899 season. During that fledgling era seven sons of a Malvern college housemaster played for the county. Like the racecourse, the cricket ground is susceptible to flooding.

Diglis River Locks are duplicated and automated, that on the east bank being the smaller, more regularly used, of the two. Downstream of the locks a new footbridge spans the river.

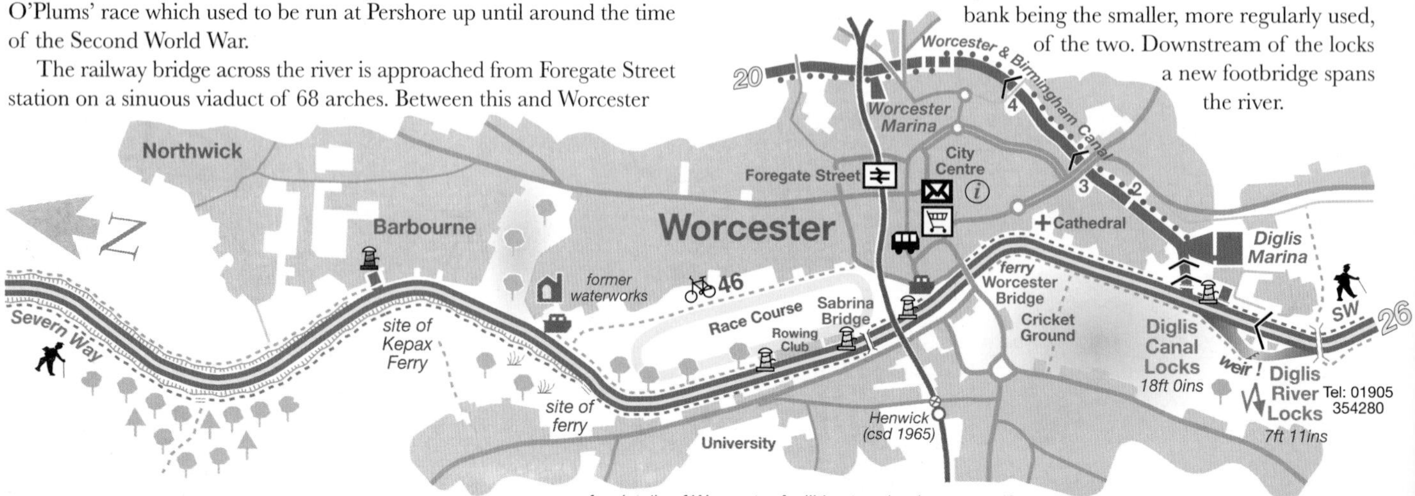

for details of Worcester facilities turn back to page 48

26 RIVER SEVERN Kempsey 4mls/0lks/1hr

LIKE a deferential waitress coming to clear the dishes, the River Teme makes little impact on the haughty Severn, but on its way down from the Welsh Marches, past Ludlow and through lush Herefordshire pastures, this lovely river hits heights of comeliness that the Severn seldom aspires to.

William Sandys, who was originally responsible for making the River Avon navigable, acquired the rights to make the Teme navigable up to Ludlow in the 17th century, but he never got around to doing anything about it. Perhaps the Civil War impeded his plans. Just a canon ball's trajectory from here the first skirmish of that conflict took place at Powick Bridge on September 23rd 1642. The Parliamentarians lost that battle but came from behind to win the war by defeating the Royalist forces on virtually the same battlefield nine years later. A long abandoned jetty hints at the former trade in oil and petroleum along the river. The long established Severn Motor Yacht Club own a nice weatherboarded clubhouse beside their private moorings just downstream of the Worcester by-pass crossing.

South of Worcester the Severn pursues an undemonstrative course. There are brief glimpses for boaters of the Malvern Hills beyond the river's high, and largely uninspiring, banks. But if the scenery momentarily falters, the novelty of deep, wide water has yet to wear off. The walker - as so often on the Severn - has the better views, not least the architectural confection that is Stanbrook Abbey, a huge Gothic Revival assemblage designed by Edward Welby Pugin, son of Augustus Welby Northmore. The abbey's nuns have recently upped sticks and moved to fresh fields in North Yorkshire, but the buildings are to gain a new lease of life as a retreat.

Kempsey comes tentatively down to the riverbank, and its substantial, squat-towered church pokes its head above the boater's eyeline. Sources vary regarding the demise of Pixham Ferry, 1939 and 1947 being the most quoted parameters. It seems, though, that a larger vessel capable of carrying vehicles was destroyed in the floods of the former, and that a rowing boat carried bravely on until the latter. There was no formal road approach to the ferry stage on the Kempsey side, so cars had to be driven across the field avoiding potholes. The Croome Hunt used the ferry and archive photographs depict the horses and hounds packed aboard the vessel. How Reynard crossed the river, is not recorded. It doesn't seem too fanciful to suppose that Sir Edward Elgar used the ferry. A keen cyclist, Kempsey is known to have been on one of his regular itineraries aboard his favourite Royal Sunbeam machine, fondly nicknamed 'Mr Phoebus'.

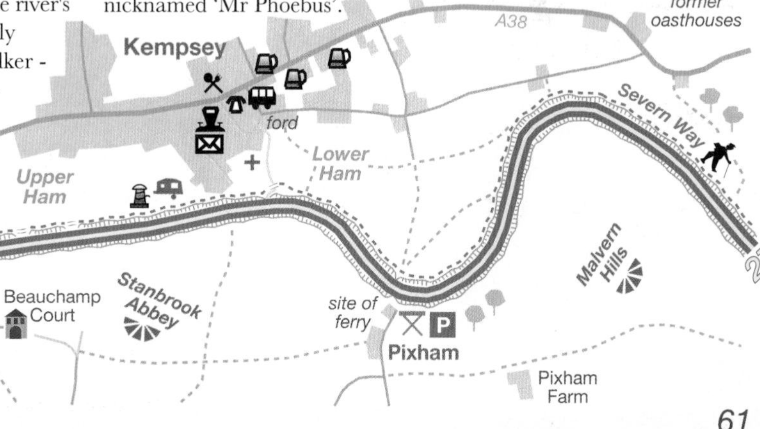

River Severn

Stourport Barge Locks

Lincomb Lock

Stourport 'Steamer'

Cormorants

Holt Castle

Worcester Warehouses

Working Barge

Lower Lode Geese Senate

Severn Way Poplars

Ashleworth Tithe Barn

Deerhurst Interior

Deerhurst Exterior

Robin Smithett

Gloucester Lock

27 RIVER SEVERN Severn Stoke 5mls/0lks/1hr

UNBRIDGED and ferry-less now, the Severn constitutes a natural obstacle all the way from Worcester's southern by-pass to Upton. Swaggering like a playground bully across its floodplain, it defies communities to get in its way, and they do their level best to not oblige; notwithstanding which, the villagers of Severn Stoke are regularly knee-deep in water. Webbed feet, though, seem a small price to pay for living in such glorious surroundings. High banks, it's true, preclude the best views from the perspective of a boat, but walkers on the Severn Way have beauty bestowed upon them in bucketfuls, the Malvern Hills being seldom out of sight, and never out of mind. The walker, too, is at liberty to pause and take things in, his counterpart at the tiller or wheel is offered no formal moorings, and those with pets aboard, used to being able to offer 'walkies' on the towpath at the drop of a hat, need to consider their pet's needs before blithely setting forth.

Outcrops of sandstone rock provide interludes of drama amidst the monotony of the river's willow-lined banks. Submerged rocks at Rhydd caused problems before the locks were built.

Two properties catch the eye: the stuccoed, crenellated, and ever so slightly pompous Severn Bank; and Severn End, whose origins can be followed back to the 15th Century, though much of it had to be rebuilt in the wake of a disastrous fire in 1896. Amusingly, it was the model for 'Brinkley Court', the country seat of Bertie Wooster's Aunt Dahlia in a number of P. G. Wodehouse's Jeeves stories. Wodehouse, it transpires, had a real aunt married to the vicar at Hanley Castle.

All the villages which hang precariously around the river's neck would once have had wharves to which the Severn's indigenous trows would trade, bringing coal from the Forest of Dean and going back with the fruit and vegetable crops of this fertile plain. But somehow we seem to have mislaid the art of making use of the river as a transport artery, preferring the impact of giant articulated lorries on the villages' roads.

It is widely known that the Malvern Hills inspired much of Elgar's music, but the Severn was also his muse: 'I am still at heart the dreamy child who used to be found in the reeds by Severn side with a sheet of paper, trying to fix the sounds and longing for something great'.

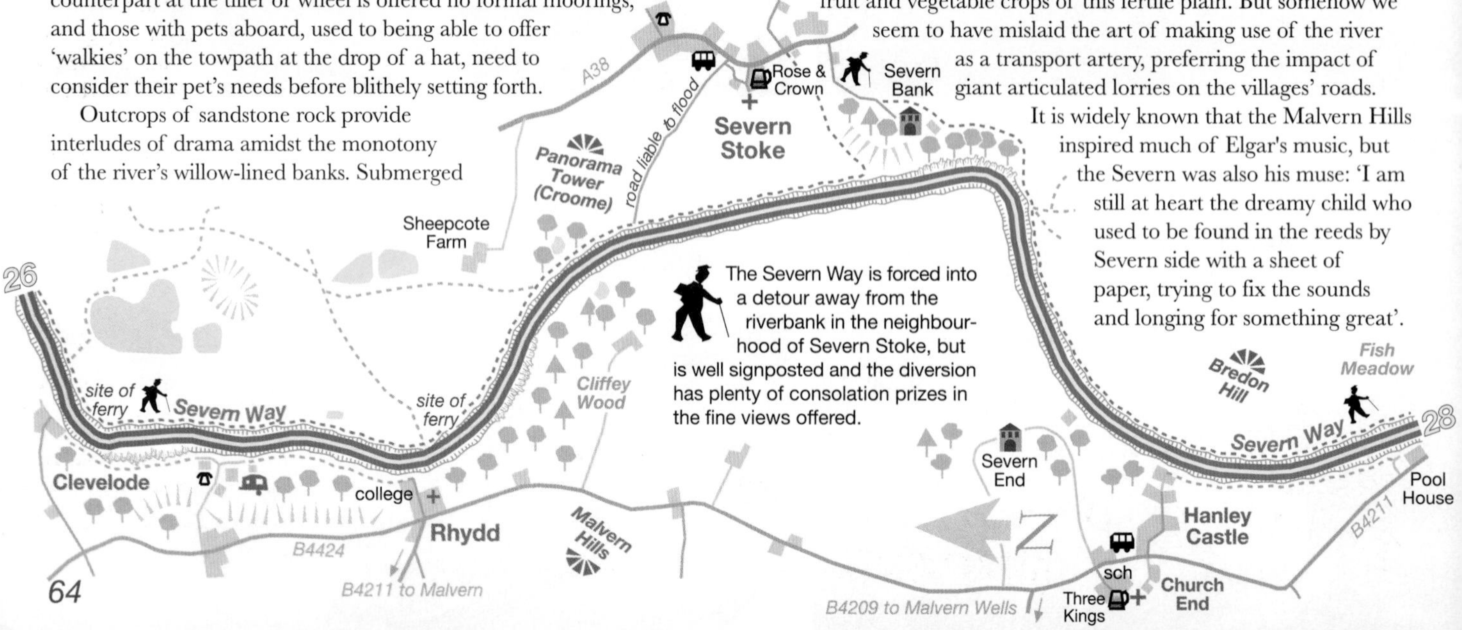

The Severn Way is forced into a detour away from the riverbank in the neighbourhood of Severn Stoke, but is well signposted and the diversion has plenty of consolation prizes in the fine views offered.

28 RIVER SEVERN Upton-upon-Severn 5mls/0lks/1hr

UPTON-UPON-SEVERN'S fleshpots come as welcome relief to the Severn's somewhat repetitive scenery, and the Severn Way swaps sides. The present bridge at Upton - which, as far as we know, has not won any prizes for its beauty - dates from the Second World War. It replaced a swing bridge, the abutments of which can still be seen. In *Worcestershire* (Robert Hale 1949) L. T. C. Rolt painted a vivid picture of watermen lingering on the cutwater embrasures of the previous bridge: 'smoking, yarning, gazing down at the smoothly flowing water, or watching the activity on the wharves'. Each plod along the road of Progress apparently rids us of something worthwhile: fords give way to ferries, ferries to swing bridges, swing bridges to fixed structures devoid of any character. And now we can travel so quickly that the average journey makes no impression on us whatsoever, all of which succinctly explains the appeal of inland waterway travel.

Upton remains a busy boating centre, with trip boats and a marina; visitor moorings are often at a premium, necessitating doubling - or even tripling - up in a manner which behoves you to be considerate neighbours. South of the town, the river arcs around the beautiful expanse of Upton Ham, 150 acres of flood plain and Lammas meadlowland, so called because cattle are put out to graze on the Ham from 1st August, Lammas Day. On the bright, mid-April day that we were undertaking our research, curlews were calling and the meadows were thickly carpeted in Lady's Smock: aka Cuckoo-flower or Milkmaids.

The bridge which carried the Tewkesbury & Malvern Railway over the Severn was equipped with a sliding central section which could be moved aside to permit tall-masted vessels to pass. The line - opened independently in 1864, but subsequently absorbed into the Midland Railway - never amounted to much more than a modest branchline, and its chief traffics appear to have been in fruit and vegetables, racing pigeons and anglers's specials. Upton became the line's western terminus when the section to Malvern was abandoned in 1952. Goods from Tewkesbury survived withdrawal of the passenger service in 1961 by three years.

One isn't sure whether to be pleased that barges are being used for a short distance between two aggregates wharves, or saddened that this activity is the sole manifestation of commercial trade on the Severn now. But give these piscatorially-named craft a wide berth if you encounter them, especially at the sharp bend at Sandy Point.

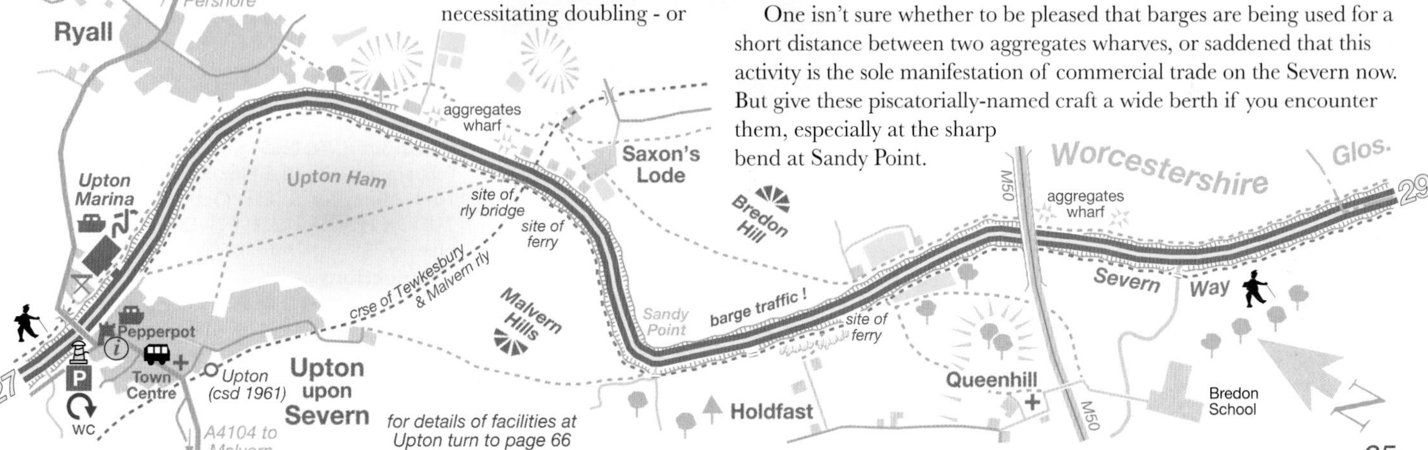

for details of facilities at Upton turn to page 66

Severn Stoke Map 27

Black and white cottages necklaced along the A38.

Eating & Drinking

ROSE & CROWN - Church Lane. Tel: 01905 371249. Half-timbered, flood-prone Marston's pub accessible from the Severn Way. WR8 9JQ

Connections

BUSES - First Midland Red services 332 & 333 to/from Worcester and Upton. Tel: 0871 200 2233.

Hanley Castle Map 27

Whilst inaccessible to boaters and walkers on the Severn Way, this charming village merits inclusion on the grounds of its historic pub, well worth taking the trouble to visit via Upton by taxi, bus or bike. Reversing the common trend, pupils from all over the district are bused into the rural High School which can trace its orgins back to the 14th century.

Eating & Drinking

THREE KINGS - Church End. Tel: 01684 592686. One of the great unspoilt pubs of England justifiably listed on CAMRA's National Inventory. Dates from the 15th century and in the same family since 1911. WR8 0BL

Connections

BUSES - service 363 to/from Worcester & Upton.

Upton-upon-Severn Map 28

They barely bother to take the bunting down in this jaunty little riverine town. What with its jazz, folk, blues, steam and water festivals there's hardly any point. Indeed, the spirit of the Severn pervades the place to such an extent that it exudes the atmosphere of a small coastal port - Upton upon Sea, perhaps, rather than upon Severn. The illusion is enhanced by the resemblance of the cupola-topped old church - known locally as The Pepperpot - to a lighthouse. Its high-spired Victorian replacement looks its best when

The 'Pepperpot'

viewed across The Ham against a backdrop of the Malvern Hills. Limited visitor pontoon moorings are provided upstream of the bridge within sight of the splendid Regal Garage with its 1930s styling, manned pumps and array of veteran recovery vehicles.

Eating & Drinking

Pubs jostle for pole position on the waterfront and it would be invidious of us to list one above another. Here, though, is a brief selection of establishments further into town:

HENRY'S - High Street. Tel: 01684 438300. Cafe with books and antiques. WR8 0HB

PUNDITS - Old Street. Tel: 01684 591022. Cosy Bangladeshi restaurant and takeaway. WR8 0HN

THE SECRET MESS - Church Street. Tel: 01684 594892. Stylish little restaurant. WR8 0HT

THRISNA - Old Street. Tel: 01684 594900. A viable alternative if Pundits is full. WR8 0HW

UPTON CHIPPY - New Street. Tel: 01684 592230. Eat in or take away fish & chips. WR8 0HR

THE WHEELHOUSE - Upton Marina. Tel: 01684 594224. Boater-friendly bar/restaurant open from 10am daily. WR8 0PB

WHITE LION HOTEL - High Street. Tel: 01684 592551. Comfortable hotel (mentioned in *Tom Jones* by Henry Fielding) with popular Brasserie. WR8 0HJ

Shopping

Inveterate travellers will make a bee-line for The Map Shop (Tel: 01684 593146) on the High Street whose wide range of maps and guide books encompasses the whole world, the *Canal Companions* included. More practically, there are Spar and Co-op convenience stores, a post office, wine merchants and a launderette (on New Street) and a Lloyds bank (open 10am-3pm Mon, Wed & Fri).

Things to Do

TOURIST INFORMATION & HERITAGE CENTRE - Church Street. Tel: 01684 594200. Housed within 'The Pepperpot'. Open 10-5 Mon-Sat (ex Thur) Apr-Sep; 10-4 Mon, Fri & Sat Oct-Mar. WR8 0HB

TUDOR HOUSE MUSEUM - Church Street. Local history & memorabilia. Tel: 01684 592447.

Connections

BUSES - services 332 and 333 operate to/from Worcester; ditto 363 which continues to Tewkesbury, and is thus useful for Severn Way walkers. Service 365 runs to/from Malvern. Tel: 0871 200 2233.

TAXIS - Upton Dial-a-Cab. Tel: 01684 593939.

29 RIVER SEVERN Tewkesbury 5mls/11k/1hr

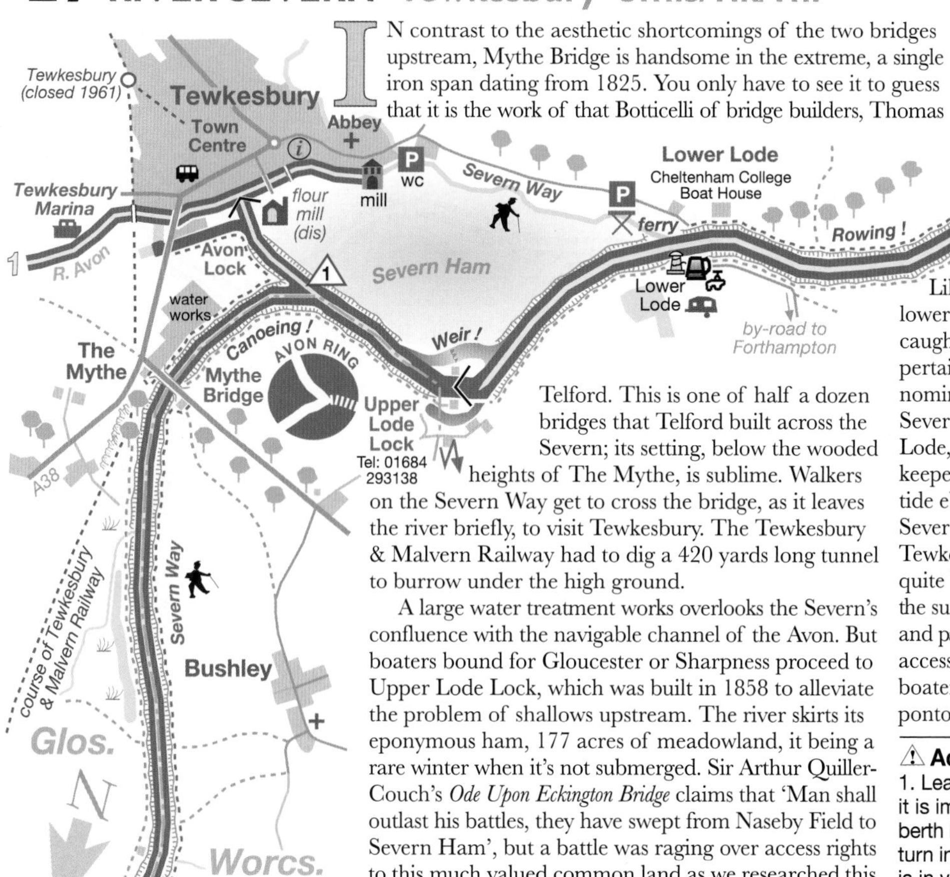

IN contrast to the aesthetic shortcomings of the two bridges upstream, Mythe Bridge is handsome in the extreme, a single iron span dating from 1825. You only have to see it to guess that it is the work of that Botticelli of bridge builders, Thomas Telford. This is one of half a dozen bridges that Telford built across the Severn; its setting, below the wooded heights of The Mythe, is sublime. Walkers on the Severn Way get to cross the bridge, as it leaves the river briefly, to visit Tewkesbury. The Tewkesbury & Malvern Railway had to dig a 420 yards long tunnel to burrow under the high ground.

A large water treatment works overlooks the Severn's confluence with the navigable channel of the Avon. But boaters bound for Gloucester or Sharpness proceed to Upper Lode Lock, which was built in 1858 to alleviate the problem of shallows upstream. The river skirts its eponymous ham, 177 acres of meadowland, it being a rare winter when it's not submerged. Sir Arthur Quiller-Couch's *Ode Upon Eckington Bridge* claims that 'Man shall outlast his battles, they have swept from Naseby Field to Severn Ham', but a battle was raging over access rights to this much valued common land as we researched this edition.

Likely as not, the keeper at Upper Lode Lock will lower you a bucket - not, disappointingly, full of freshly caught elvers - but containing a useful instruction sheet pertaining to the passage downstream. Though nominally a freshwater river above Gloucester, the Severn can be tidal on 'high springs' as far as Upper Lode, and even occasionally beyond. At such times the keeper may advise you to proceed no further until the tide ebbs. A second channel of the Avon enters the Severn at Lower Lode, from where the view of Tewkesbury Abbey, with Bredon Hill as a backdrop, is quite breathtaking. A passenger ferry operates here in the summer months and is popular with walkers, cyclists and patrons of the Lower Lode Hotel. How sad it is that access to Deerhurst and its Saxon church is denied the boater; it is hard to imagine the cost of a mooring pontoon would prove prohibitive.

⚠ Advice for Boaters

1. Leaving or entering the Severn, for or from the Avon, it is important to avoid the sandbar. Give this a wide berth by keeping over towards the southern bank as you turn into the Avon, or by making sure that Mythe Bridge is in view before turning upstream into the Severn.

for details of Tewkesbury see Map 1

30 RIVER SEVERN Apperley & Ashleworth 6mls/0lks/1hr

PASSING villages so reluctant to dip their toes into the flood plain of the Severn that they hang half a mile back from its banks, the river suddenly finds itself baulked by the high flank of Wainlode Hill. Erosion has carved a bluff grey rockface here, rising sheer from the water's edge like a seaside cliff. The deep water channel hugs the northern bank and old barges have been beached on the south side to prevent further incursions into the river's bank. The River Chelt sidles in from the east. Nearby is the ruined entrance lock of the Coombe Hill Canal, built to carry Forest of Dean coal to the spa town of Cheltenham, though it never actually got that far and was abandoned as early as 1876. Following more than a century of graceful decay, the canal is now administered by the Gloucestershire Wildlife Trust as a linear nature reserve, the sequestered, pollarded-willowed haunt of curlews, hen harriers and goshawks.

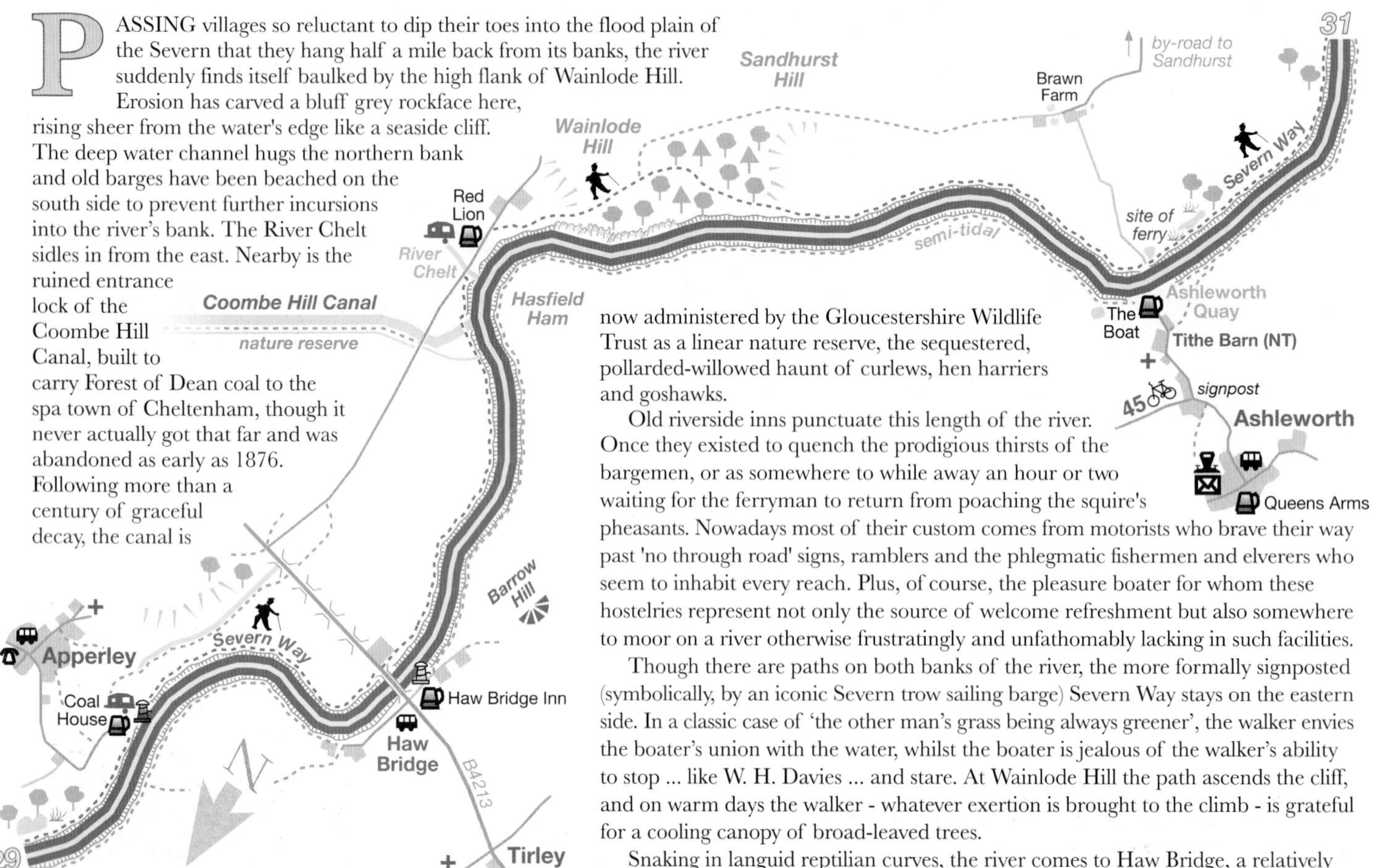

Old riverside inns punctuate this length of the river. Once they existed to quench the prodigious thirsts of the bargemen, or as somewhere to while away an hour or two waiting for the ferryman to return from poaching the squire's pheasants. Nowadays most of their custom comes from motorists who brave their way past 'no through road' signs, ramblers and the phlegmatic fishermen and elverers who seem to inhabit every reach. Plus, of course, the pleasure boater for whom these hostelries represent not only the source of welcome refreshment but also somewhere to moor on a river otherwise frustratingly and unfathomably lacking in such facilities.

Though there are paths on both banks of the river, the more formally signposted (symbolically, by an iconic Severn trow sailing barge) Severn Way stays on the eastern side. In a classic case of 'the other man's grass being always greener', the walker envies the boater's union with the water, whilst the boater is jealous of the walker's ability to stop ... like W. H. Davies ... and stare. At Wainlode Hill the path ascends the cliff, and on warm days the walker - whatever exertion is brought to the climb - is grateful for a cooling canopy of broad-leaved trees.

Snaking in languid reptilian curves, the river comes to Haw Bridge, a relatively modern structure dating from 1961, having replaced an early 19th century bridge demolished by the tanker barge *Darleydale*. Sailing 'in ballast', and thus high in the water, downstream, its wheelhouse collided with the bridge and the tanker skipper was killed.

This is Ivor Gurney country, the Gloucestershire poet and composer whose nerves never fully recovered from their exposure to the maelstrom of the trenches. The Severn was an important source of inspiration, as his first book of poetry *Severn & Somme*, published in 1917, confirms. In his following volume *War's Embers* the poem 'Above Ashleworth' appears, which speaks of the 'steady Severn silver and grey'. That, at least, hasn't changed. Another 'local' writer worth seeking out is Brian Waters, whose *Severn Tide* (J. M. Dent 1947) is a poetic evocation of a riparian way of life largely vanished.The stagnant ponds which accompany the river between Ashleworth and Sandhurst are where clay was dug to make bricks.

Lower Lode — Map 29

LOWER LODE INN - Tel: 01684 293224. A Canal & River Trust mooring pontoon provides access to this rambling riverside inn which operates an outboard-engined ferry across to the Tewkesbury bank during the summer months. Bar and restaurant food, B&B, and a good choice of locally sourced real ales. GL19 4RE

Chaceley Stock — Map 29

Riverside hamlet a mile east of Chaceley itself. Elver and bacon omelette is apparently a local delicacy. YEW TREE INN - Tel: 01452 780333. Isolated riverside inn at site of Deerhurst ferry. Generously portioned, home made food. Doom Bar and guest ales. Apartment for let. Pontoon moorings exclusively for customers. GL19 4EQ

Apperley — Map 30

Once a village known for apple growing and salmon fishing, Apperley now exists chiefly as a commuter base for folk who work in Gloucester and Cheltenham and there is no longer enough daytime activity to support a shop.

Eating & Drinking

THE COAL HOUSE - riverside with pontoon moorings exclusively for patrons .Tel: 01452 780211. Steak on the Stone is their signature dish. Apartment for let. GL17 4DN

Connections

BUSES - service 351, operated by Swanbrook Coaches, links Apperley approx bi-hourly Mon-Sat with Gloucester and Tewkesbury, a highly enjoyable ride in its own right, never mind its usefulness to Severn Way walkers. Tel: 0871 200 2233.

Haw Bridge — Map 30

Macabre scene, in 1938, of the yet unsolved 'Cheltenham Torso Murder Mystery' concerning a retired army captain, whose headless and limbless body was found in the river by fishermen; his lover, a male dancer who subsequently committed suicide; and the latter's mother, an illegal abortionist!

Eating & Drinking

HAW BRIDGE INN - riverside to south of bridge. Tel: 01452 780316. A convivial Wadworth pub which benefits from both private and Canal & River Trust pontoon moorings. GL19 4HJ

RED LION - riverside but *no* easy mooring. Tel: 01452 730935. What Severn Way walkers lose over Ashleworth, they gain with this charming brick-built inn at the foot of Wainlode Hill. Wickwar ales, bar and restaurant meals. Camping to rear. GL2 9LW

Connections

BUSES - service 351, operated by Swanbrook Coaches, links Haw Bridge approx bi-hourly Mon-Sat with Gloucester, and Tewkesbury. Tel: 0871 200 2233.

Ashleworth — Map 30

There no longer being a ferry, walkers on the Severn Way are denied access to heavenly Ashleworth. Follow the lane inland from the pub and you'll quickly come upon Ashleworth's magnificent Tithe Barn cared for by the National Trust. Past that stands Ashleworth Court, built of blue lias and dating from 1460. Frustratingly it's in private hands, but tucked away between it and the Tithe Barn is the village's splendid church of St Andrew & Bartholomew. The interior is utterly charming, though we're not sure, given the temptations of The Boat - that we would readily subscribe to the wall-painted advice in the South Aisle to be 'there fore sober and watch unto prayer'. Preaching cross on the village green.

Eating & Drinking

THE BOAT - riverside, mooring pontoon for customers. Tel: 01452 700272. Celebrated pub which has been owned by the same family for generations. Catering, formerly limited to lunchtime rolls, has been upgraded of late, and basket meals and burgers are now available, the ideal accompaniment to an ever-changing quartet of for the most part locally brewed ales. No unnecessary noise, just the soft congenial burr of Gloucestershire voices. Humbly yet beautifully appointed, with fine old photographs of elvering and the long gone ferry on the walls. GL19 4HZ

31 RIVER SEVERN Gloucester 4mls/11k/1hr

LONG Reach leads to Upper Parting. These old river names have an evocative resonance. And there were deeper subtleties: the navigable channel downstream of the Parting was known to working boatmen as 'Skipper's Length', whilst that above was known as 'Mates'. The tradition was that barge skippers would be at the wheel for the tortuous, narrow exit channel from Gloucester, being relieved by the mate once Upper Parting had been reached .

The now unnavigable western channel of the Severn, which loops past the village of Maisemore, was used to gain access to the Herefordshire & Gloucestershire Canal, a 34 mile rural waterway which took fifty years to build. Within forty years of completion in 1845 it had largely been converted into a railway. Twenty years ago no one would have considered that the H & G could ever be made navigable again, but other 'impossible' restoration projects have been achieved, and 'never' is no longer a word in any self-respecting canal activist's vocabulary. In recent years the junction basin at Over has been restored, though being on a tidal reach of the Severn it cannot be accessed by inland waterway craft. The Wharf House, however, has been transformed into a visitor centre and restaurant (with rooms) and boat trips are operated along a short length of the canal extended in 2012.

⚠ Advice for Boaters

1. On reaching Upper Parting, boaters are encouraged to telephone ahead to the lock-keeper at Gloucester - Tel: 01452 310832 - so that the lock into Gloucester Docks can be made ready for them.
2. Approaching Gloucester Lock beware the current drawing you towards the unnavigable channel to Lower Parting. The quay wall to your left has chains through which a line should be looped until the green light signals that you can enter the lock. Attach your stern line first.

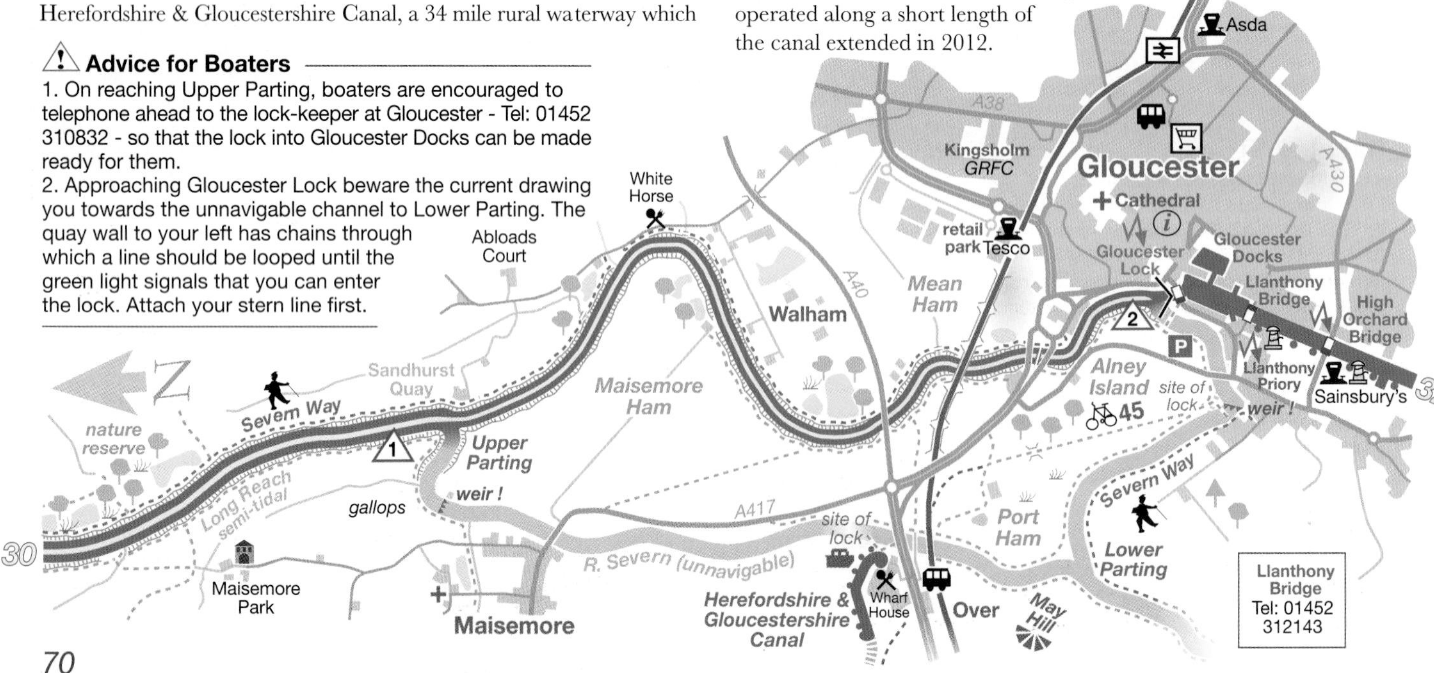

The navigable, eastern channel of the Severn must have demanded all the barge skipper's fund of experience. If you have been used to the motorway breadth of the river down from Tewkesbury, this B-road backwater comes as something of a shock. It forms a surreptitious approach to the city, for the overhanging willows hide any view which might otherwise be had of the cathedral, but in its favour lies the fact that it ushers you into the very centre of the city without experiencing any of the drab outskirts which form an introduction to most towns and cities.

A series of bridges span the river as roads and railways converge on the city centre, before you reach the long wall of the old River Quay, where vessels which had navigated the tidal Severn used to berth prior to the development of the docks and the ship canal from Sharpness. Downstream of The Quay the river branches again, the right hand unnavigable channel leading round to Lower Parting. Head instead for Gloucester Lock, which dates from 1812 and was originally in the form of a staircase pair. Now it is one deep chamber, mechanised and spanned by a liftbridge carrying a busy road around the docks. As the lock fills, Gloucester Docks are gradually revealed in all their grandeur and it is with a sense of exhilaration that you proceed into the Main Basin to seek out a mooring amidst these splendid surroundings.

Cargo-handling may be history, but the docks retain considerable appeal. And if the handsome warehouses house council departments now in place of wheat and maize and barley, and if there are more students than stevedores, there is still much to exercise the imagination. In certain lights the setting can be seen as Atkinson Grimshaw - the Yorkshire bred Victorian artist, much given to atmospheric dockland scenes - must have been inspired by: his finished canvas hangs in the city's recently renovated Art Gallery. A particular favourite of ours is the Mariners' Chapel, erected in 1849 to care for the spiritual needs of the docks' itinerant and international population of seamen. The interior is usually open to visitors and a service is held each Sunday at 3pm. Ivor Gurney was the chapel's organist before the Great War.

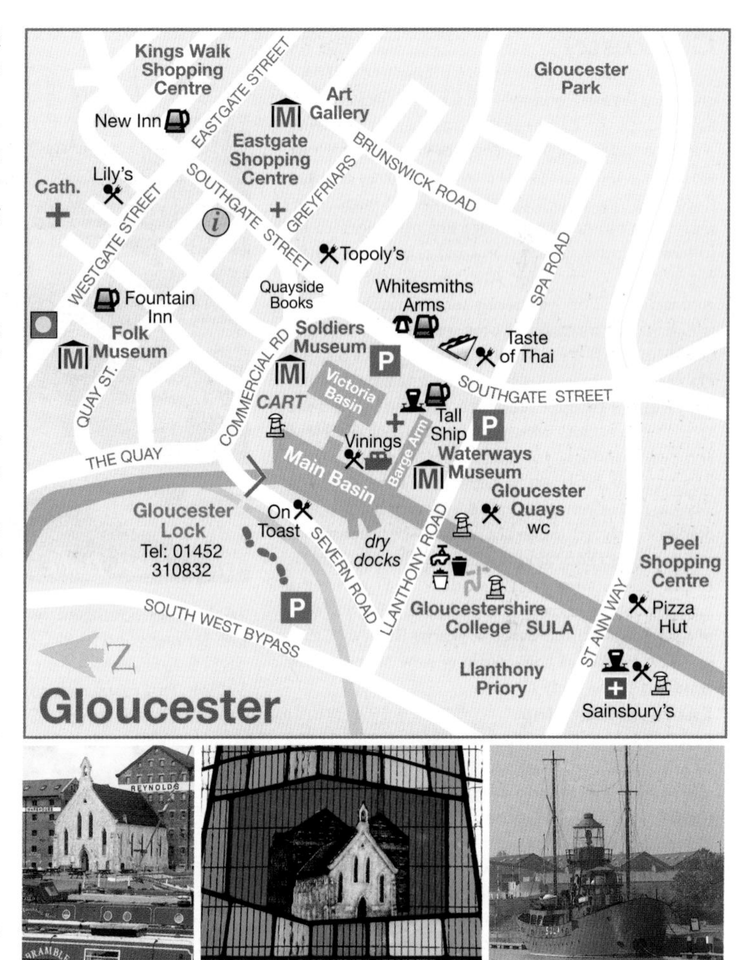

Gloucester Map 31

Seagulls reinforce the maritime ambience of this charming 'West Country' city. Charles Dickens was amazed to find merchant seamen wandering conspicuously along the streets of what he imagined would be a quiet cathedral city. He followed one and discovered 'endless intricacies of dock and huge three-masted ships'. Naturally, there are no sailors to be followed today, and, in any case, one has one's reputation to consider. Also, most users of this guidebook will be wondering what Gloucester *itself* is like, having already become acquainted with the docks. In truth it's a bit of a curate's egg, a bit of a Mahler symphony, consisting of serene passages and alleyways interspersed with strident concrete shopping precincts which could be anywhere. Here and there, though, you encounter evidence of the Roman 'Glevum', stressing Gloucester's longevity. The city has, however, in its cathedral, a masterpiece of medieval architecture, an act of faith which transcends the perceived shortcomings of modern life. Here is the largest stained glass window in England, the intricate fan vaulting of the cloisters, and the tomb of King Edward II, murdered at nearby Berkeley Castle in 1327. Seek out the ravishing new Ivor Gurney windows in the Lady Chapel.

Eating & Drinking

FOUNTAIN INN - Westgate Street. Tel: 01452 522562. *Good Beer Guide* recommended 17th century inn within a stone's throw of the docks. GL1 2NW

LILY'S - College Court. Tel: 01452 307060. Comfortable and quaint, cathedral-side tea room and restaurant in the Keith Goss mould. GL1 2NJ

ON TOAST - The Docks. Tel: 01452 505440. Modern cafe and take-away beside the main basin where just about everything is served either in or on toast ... including Mars Bars! GL1 2LE

Gloucester Docks & Cathedral

TALL SHIP - Southgate. Tel: 01452 522793. Dockland pub serving good food. GL1 2EX

TASTE OF THAI - Southgate Street. Tel: 01452 520894. Thai restaurant adjacent dockland. GL1 1UT

TOPOLY'S - Southgate Street. Tel: 01452 331062. Atmospheric Italian near the docks. GL1 1TX

VININGS - Docks. Tel: 01452 384455. Pan Asian buffet overlooking the main basin. GL1 2EG

WHARF HOUSE - Over. Tel: 01452 332900. Restaurant/rooms operated by the H&GCT. GL2 8DB

WHITE HORSE - Sandhurst Road. Tel: 01452 414651. Former out of town riverside pub transformed into a Chinese restaurant. GL2 9NG

WHITESMITHS ARMS - Southgate. Tel: 01452 312947. Congenial Arkell's pub adjacent docks. GL1 1UR

Shopping

The Gloucester Quays development on the south side of the docks hosts an unnervingly wide range of designer outlets ... *designed* to wreak havoc on your bank balance. Sainsbury's are well placed for boaters by High Orchard Bridge. Gloucester Antiques Centre is opposite the Waterways Museum on Llanthony Road. Quayside Books & Prints on Commercial Road often has some inland waterway items. Gloucester Brewery shop adjacent Waterways Museum.

Things to Do

TOURIST INFORMATION - 28 Southgate Street. Tel: 01452 396572. GL1 2DP

GLOUCESTER WATERWAYS MUSEUM - Llanthony Warehouse. Tel: 01452 318200. Admission charge. Boat trips on the G&S Canal. GL1 2EH

SOLDIERS OF GLOUCESTERSHIRE MUSEUM - The Docks. Tel: 01452 522682. Local heroism commemorated in the former Custom House. Key displays concerning 'The Glosters' defiance during the Korean War. GL1 2HE

CITY MUSEUM & ART GALLERY - Brunswick Road. Tel: 01452 396131. GL1 1HP

GLOUCESTER FOLK MUSEUM - Westgate. Tel: 01452 396868. Interesting exhibits on local industries and Severn fishing techniques. GL1 2PG

TAILOR OF GLOUCESTER - College Green. Tel: 01452 422856. Beatrix Potter museum/shop. GL1 2NJ

SULA - Tel: 01452 527566. Retired lightship run as a Buddhist/holistic centre. Gift shop and tours.

Connections

BUSES - useful links with Tewkesbury (71/35) and Stroud (66) etc. Tel: 0871 200 2233.

TRAINS - services to/from Birmingham (Cross-Country), London and Bristol and through the Golden Valley (Great Western). Tel: 03457 484950.

TAXIS - Central Taxis. Tel: 01452 382020.

Near Purton

Gloucester & Sharpness

32 GLOUCESTER & SHARPNESS CANAL Quedgeley 4mls/0lks/1hr

STRIDING confidently out of the county town, the Gloucester & Sharpness Canal certainly exudes the air of a commercial waterway, one on which you might confidently - not to say nervously - anticipate a close encounter with an ocean-going vessel at any given moment. Alas, such apprehensions are unfounded, there has been no coastal trade, to speak of, up to Gloucester for thirty years. New housing estates are burgeoning beside the canal and the industries which once relied upon water transport have forgotten its existence. Solely the occasional convolvulus-strangled bollard, or the fact that railway lines remain embedded in the towpath suggest that serious commerce was once enacted here.

What was originally known as the Gloucester & Berkeley Ship Canal (for it was to be two miles longer than as finished, and destined to rejoin the Severn estuary at Berkeley Pill) was promoted in the *fin de siecle* years of the 18th century to by-pass the treacherous shallows and mercurial tides of the lower Severn. In common with the majority of engineering projects - right up to the present day - it took much more money and much more time to complete than was initially envisaged ... thirty years in fact. Its original engineer, Robert Mylne was sacked, and it fell to the ubiquitous Master Telford to finish it.

For a century and a half the canal more than adequately fulfilled its function. Not until we perversely concentrated the carriage of goods on the most environmentally unsound means at mankind's disposal was it rendered obsolete.

Hempsted is the first of many keeper-operated swing bridges which span the canal at regular intervals. Most* of them lack sufficient headroom for even low-slung pleasure craft, but the rumour mill usually works well and they appear to open for your passage as if by magic. Mobile phone apps are being trialled to see if the keepers may ultimately (though sadly) be replaced by technology. Some two miles out, the canal has been rerouted to facilitate the construction of a new road and features a massive new swing-bridge

Rea Bridge is graced by an ornately classical keeper's house, notable for its Doric-columned portico. These charming structures are to become increasingly familiar as the canal journeys south. North of Sellars Bridge the canal widens at the site of an oil terminal which received supplies by coastal vessels trading from South Wales until the early 1980s. The former quay remains intact, and, in a nice gesture to the maritime past, roads in the new waterside housing estate are named after vessels which once plied the canal.

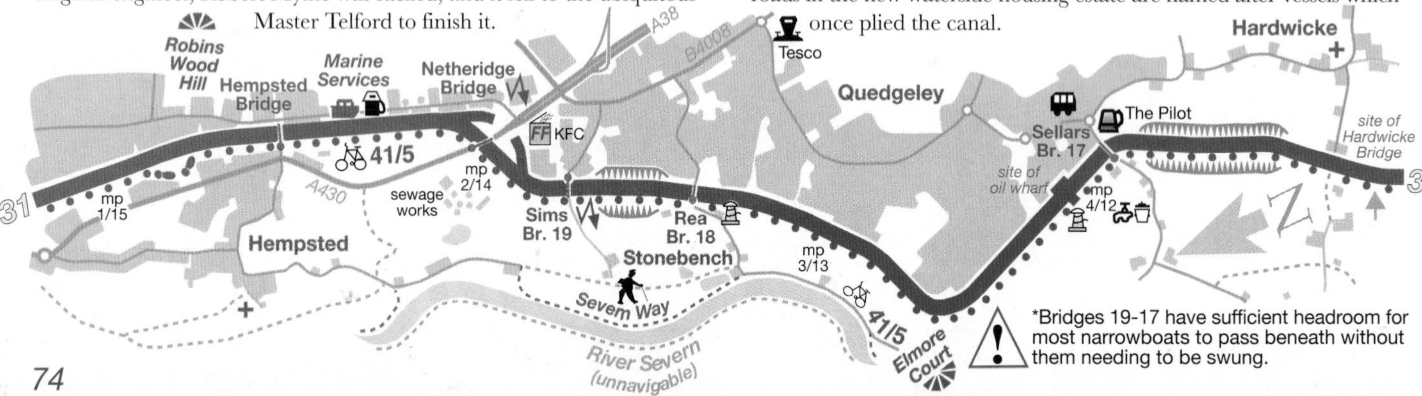

33 GLOUCESTER & SHARPNESS CANAL Saul Junction 4mls/0lks/1hr

ACCOMPANIED - though never overshadowed - by pylons and power lines, the Gloucester & Sharpness Canal traverses an apparently remote, low-slung landscape lost in a topographical void between the Cotswolds and the Forest of Dean. The fields focus on farms which, in their loneliness - and yours - assume a heightened significance. Between Parkend Bridge and Saul Junction the waterway is slightly elevated above the surrounding countryside with echoes of East Anglia in its reedy margins and reflections of high, wide skies. A derelict dumb barge lies moored listlessly to the towpath with an ersatz cargo of reeds and water: its wheelhouse has inexplicably vanished since the previous edition.

Saul Junction will once again be able to live up to its name when (and if!) the ambitious Cotswold Canals restoration project is realised - see Map 36. The Stroudwater Canal predated the G&S by almost fifty years and was formally abandoned in 1954, though trade had ceased a dozen years earlier.

Pending restoration, the junction is still a fascinating location, recently lent added prominence by the creation of a sizeable marina. The Cotswold Canal Trust have a heritage centre and trip boat at Saul and the Willow Trust also operate a pair of trip boats for the disabled. Car parks bring landborne visitors and Wycliffe College come here to row. So, all in all, there's rarely a dull moment. We would recommend the reedy towpath of the Stroudwater Canal down to Framilode.

At Fretherne Bridge you encounter a sizeable canalside flour mill which, in a previous existence, belonged to Cadburys. Coal came in by ship from South Wales, whilst waterborne trade between here and the company's other premises at Blackpole (Map 20) and Bournville (Map 15) was once intensive; the last cargo of chocolate 'crumb' being carried from Frampton to Bournville by narrowboat circa 1961.

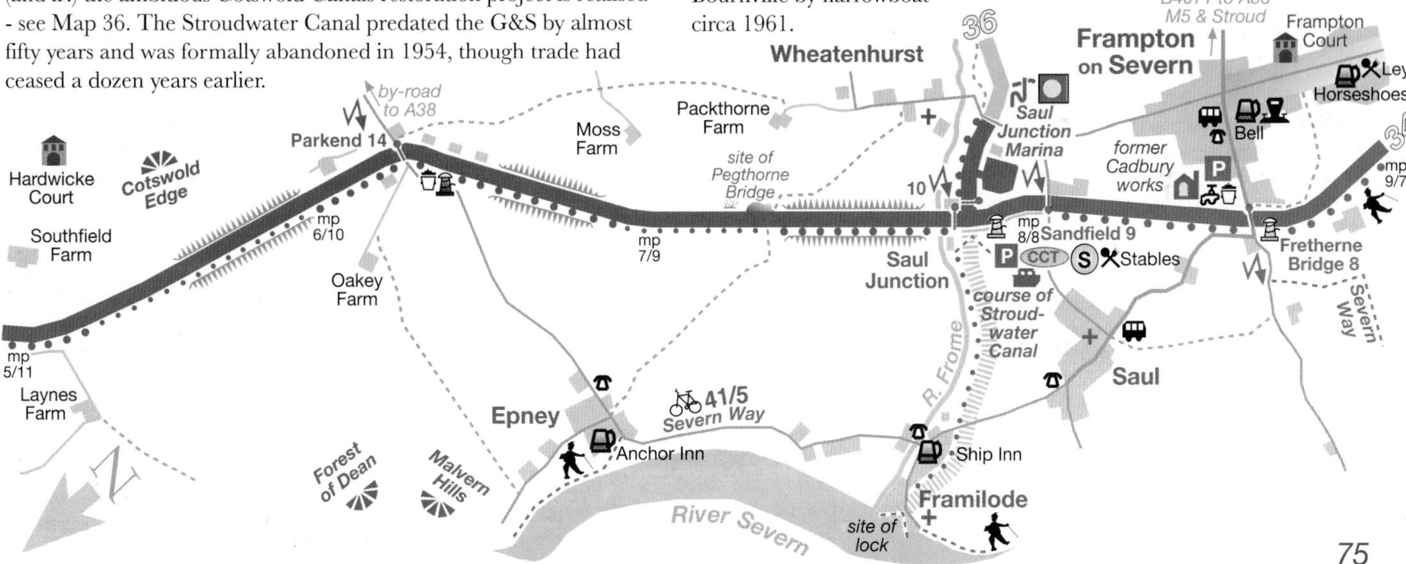

Splatt Bridge

Frampton-on-Severn Map 33

Frampton reminds you of another village grouped haphazardly about an extensive green on another extremity of the inland waterways - Nun Monkton on the Yorkshire Ouse. Exiles and Anglophiles fantasise about villages like Frampton where Fair Rosamund - Henry II's mistress - is reputed to have been born. Rosamund's Green incorporates a cricket pitch, duckponds and an array of horse chestnuts overlooked by a heterogeneous collection of houses from the large to the small, from the merely heavenly to the inherently sublime. Peacocks call from the 18th century purlieus of Frampton Court (which offers accommodation - Tel: 01452 740698) and many of the trees on the green have circular seats mandatorily made for watching the world go by. An avenue of chestnuts known locally as 'The Narles' leads to the church of St Mary the Virgin.

Eating & Drinking

THE BELL INN - The Green. Tel: 01452 740346. Bistro, fish restaurant, afternoon teas and accommodation. Overlooks the cricket pitch. GL2 7EP

LEY BISTRO - The Green. Tel: 01452 740077. Pretty little cafe and restaurant open daily (ex Mon) for breakfasts, coffees, lunches and teas. GL2 7DY

THREE HORSESHOES - The Green. Tel: 01452 742100. Convivial *Good Beer Guide* listed local with boule pitch to the rear. Home made food, Uley bitter brewed nearby. Flagstoned bar. GL2 7DY

Shopping

Excellent new-build timber shop called, appropriately enough 'The Green Shop' offering a mouth-watering range of provisions plus hot snacks for hungry walkers.

Connections

BUSES - minimalist weekday commuter service 14A/113 to/from Gloucester. Tel: 0871 200 2233.
TAXIS - Saul Taxis. Tel: 01453 826763

Framilode Map 33

A 'blowy, Severn-tided place' in the words of Ivor Gurney who kept his sailing boat *Dorothy* here. His poem *The Lock Keeper* concerns the lifestyle of the contemporary incumbent, James Harris. A good location to see the Severn Bore: *www.severn-bore.co.uk*

Eating & Drinking

THE SHIP INN - Tel: 01452 740260. Charming pub beside a reedy length of the former Stroudwater Canal. Good food, local ales and accommodation. GL2 7LH

Saul Map 33

Shopless, publess, but not devoid of interest, particularly in that a number of its houses feature unusual friezes above their front doors. The name isn't biblical, but derived, rather, from the French for willow - *saule*. The Cotswold Canals Trust have one of their admirable visitor centres alongside CART's services block at Saul Junction - Tel: 0785 402 6504 - the other's at Stroud. Also, nice little cafe called The Stables (Tel: 01452 741965 - GL2 7LA) by Sandfield Swing Bridge.

Slimbridge Map 34

The village straggles down from the A38 to Shepherd's Patch, beyond which the road crosses the canal swing-bridge and makes a bee-line for the Wetlands Trust.

Eating & Drinking

TUDOR ARMS - adjacent Patch Bridge. Tel: 01453 890306. Country inn with a good choice of bar and restaurant meals. Beers from Uleys, Wadworth and Wye Valley. Bed & Breakfast. GL2 7BP

Things to Do

SLIMBRIDGE WETLAND CENTRE - half a mile north-west of Patch Bridge. Tel: 01453 891900. Open daily year round, Slimbridge has the world's largest collection of rare and endangered ducks, geese and swans and offers brilliant views across the Severn from its observation tower. GL2 7BT

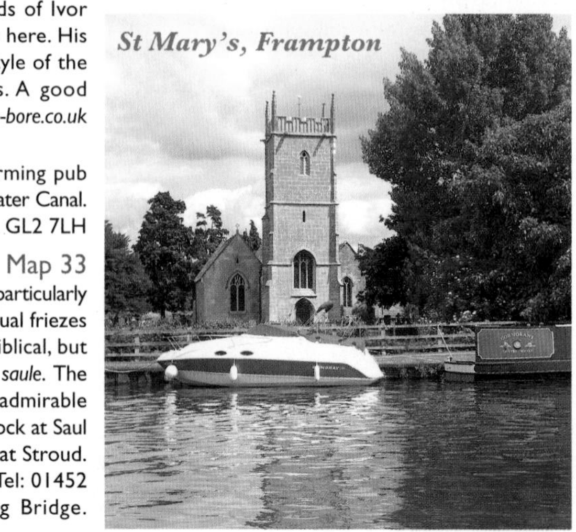
St Mary's, Frampton

34 GLOUCESTER & SHARPNESS CANAL Slimbridge 4mls/0lks/1hr

HAVING acquired the mantle of the 'Severn Way', the canal continues its delightfully bucolic progress, making its way past willow-fringed dykes draining fields extending down to the flood bank of the Severn; a seething, boiling mass of cafeteria tea-coloured water at high tide. Frampton's isolated parish church overlooks Splatt Bridge, which is followed by the entrance point to the once partially navigable River Cam, now used simply as a feeder to the canal. A common feature of the Gloucester & Sharpness from the 1930s onwards were shanties. Built initially as holiday homes, many were gradually upgraded for domestic use throughout the year. Often self-built by their owners on land owned by the Sharpness Dock Company, some were actually constructed from materials brought along the canal by barge. Once there were almost a hundred of them, now less than half a dozen remain inhabited.

To the north-west, far beyond the Severn, lies the landmark of May Hill (971ft), topped by a prominent clump of pine, planted to commemorate Victoria's Golden Jubilee. May Day is traditionally welcomed in on its summit by Morris dancers and the composer Gerald Finzi's ashes were scattered on its summit in 1973, seventeen years after his death.

Slimbridge is derived from 'slyme bridge', a reference to the once marshy nature of the surrounding landscape. The New Grounds are exactly that, land reclaimed from the river's tidal grasp during the 16th and 17th centuries. They provide rich pastures for cattle and once featured a number of decoys for the catching of duck. Nowadays, of course, it is with the preservation of duck and wildfowl that the area is concerned, since Peter Scott's establishment here of the Slimbridge Wildfowl and Wetland Trust in 1946. Son of the famous Antarctic explorer, Sir Peter Scott was the original Vice-President of the Inland Waterways Association, a close friend of Robert Aickman and one time husband of the novelist and early IWA secretary Elizabeth Jane Howard. In the early days of the Wildfowl Trust Peter Scott brought a converted narrowboat called *Beatrice* to Shepherd's Patch to provide accommodation for visiting ornithologists. In 1950 *Beatrice* undertook a lengthy voyage of the northern canals as vividly described by Robert Aickman in *The River Runs Uphill.*

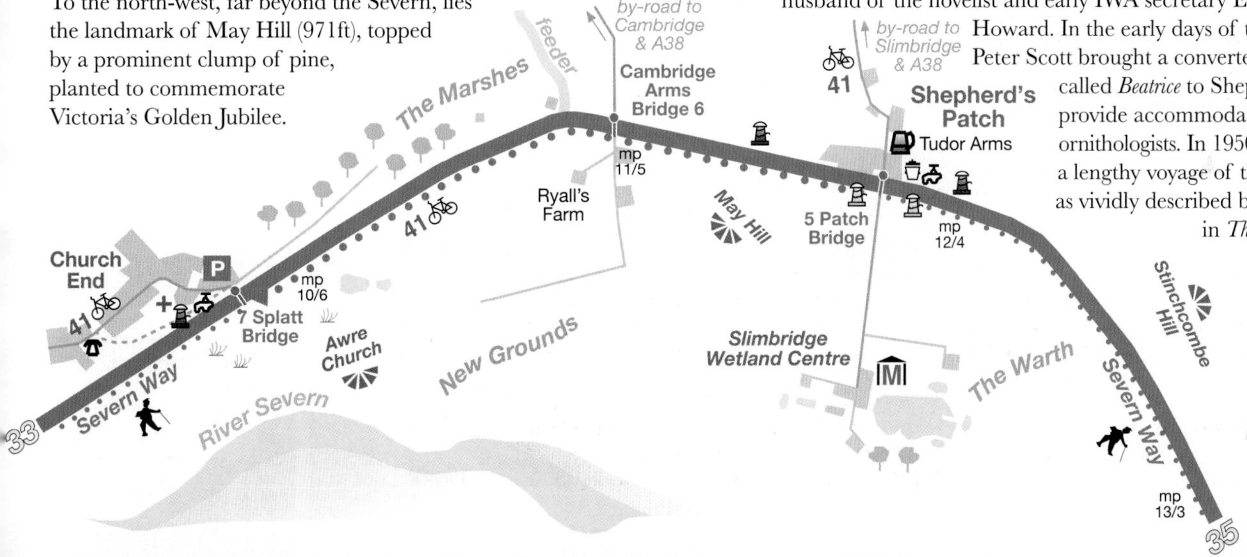

Gloucester & Sharpness

1 Little & Large @ Purton
2 Sharpness Docks
3 Purton Hulk
4 Sharpness Ponies
5 Purton Memorial
6 Saul Junction
7 Reedbed Barge
8 Purton Tiller
9 Mile 'Peg'
10 Quedgeley Goose

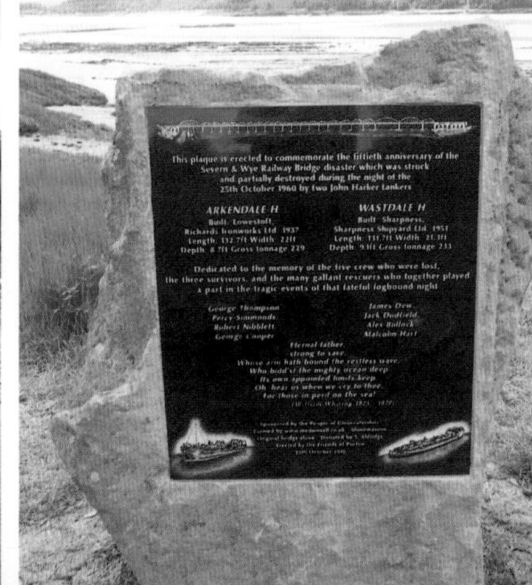

35 GLOUCESTER & SHARPNESS CANAL Sharpness 3mls/0lks/1hr

THE canal moves languorously through a landscape which feels as if it's about to fall off the edge of the globe. In the old days, perhaps, map-makers would have written "here be monsters" beyond the floodbank of the Severn: for all its proximity, the Forest of Dean might as well be on another planet.

Presently the canal curves round to Purton past a treatment plant which extracts its water on behalf of the population of Bristol. A pair of swing bridges (operated by a single keeper at the lower bridge who uses CCTV) span the waterway as it winds around to the very edge of the Severn.

There will be those in your party whose ears prick up at the mention of Purton's hulks, excited by the image of a community populated by muscular young men. When we first passed along the canal in the convivial company of Healings bargemen, learning aurally of the Purton wrecks, we marvelled for an innocent moment that such a small and back of beyond place should boast a cinema. Intending no slur on the males currently resident in the neighbourhood, both assumptions are wide of the mark, and the 'Friends of Purton' will put you right, for they are a group devoted to the preservation and interpretation of upwards of eighty abandoned vessels - trows, schooners, barges, lighters - beached on Purton's shoreline to combat erosion. Painstakingly, each historic vessel has been identified and had its key dates itemised, the result being an open air 'museum' of no little poignancy and resonance.

Savouring panoramic views of the Severn estuary, you reach the remains of a swing bridge, which once carried a railway; not only over the canal, but over to the far side of the Severn as well! Opened in 1879, primarily to carry Forest of Dean coal across to Sharpness Docks, it consisted of twenty-one fixed arches spanning the estuary and a moveable arch, propelled by steam, over the canal. The cylindrical base of the moveable arch, together with a couple of masonry arches on the opposite bank, are this astonishing structure's sole remnants, though an interpretive panel and adjacent model help to envisage how impressive it must have looked. During the Second World War, apparently, practising RAF pilots were in the dare-devil habit of flying *beneath* the bridge.

On a fog-bound October evening in 1960, *Arkendale* and *Wastdale*, two Harker petrol barges heading for Gloucester, missed the entrance to Sharpness Docks and collided with the bridge, demolishing one of the piers and bringing two

continued overleaf:

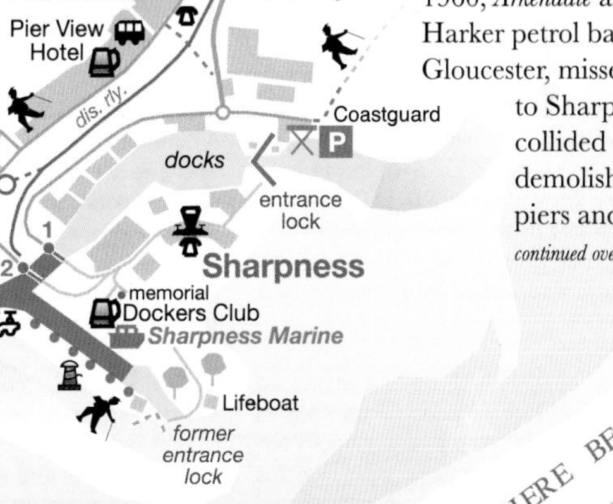

continued from page 79:

of its girder spans down on themselves. Their unstable cargoes ignited, and the blaze was worsened by the severing of a gas main on the bridge itself. Eyewitnesses described how the whole river was set alight. There were five fatalities from the barges, but things could have been worse, a group of contractors working on the bridge had clocked off early to listen to a Henry Cooper boxing bout on the radio. The railway, alas, never re-opened, and the remains of the two barges still lie off Purton.

So it would have been nice to know Sharpness when Tom and Angela Rolt moored *Cressy* here for 'a memorable month of summer' in 1948, and to have shared with them their train rides over the bridge to Lydney and the Forest of Dean. At that time there was considerable petroleum tanker barge traffic between Avonmouth and Worcester and Stourport, together with the occasional passage of a coastal vessel bound for Gloucester. Over the intervening half century cargoes ebbed and flowed almost as furiously as the Severn itself, but the last regular through traffic was in the shape of Healing's barges which plied between Avonmouth and Tewkesbury until 1998.

Yet the docks live on, operated now by the Victoria Group, whose portfolio also includes Boston (Lincs), Bromborough (Wirral), Plymouth, and Seaham (Co. Durham). Annual tonnage is in the region of a healthy half a million - fertilizer from France, Germany and North Africa; cement from northern Spain; timber, paper, coal, wheat and grain - though perhaps it neatly illustrates shortcomings in our balance of trade and manufacturing prowess that exports are restricted to scrap metal. Ships of up to 6000 tonnes are able to pass through the entrance lock - which has dimensions of 320 feet long by 57 feet wide - and if you want to see them you should position yourself at the picnic site on the south side of the approach jetty about half an hour before high water. The celebrated excursion vessels *Waverley* and *Balmoral* occasionally call at Sharpness during the summer months.

The original course of the canal veers to the right, making its approach to the former entrance lock along an arm now used for moorings. Here, between 1939 and 1966 was berthed the mercantile training ship *Vindicatrix*, celebrated by a memorial near the Dockers Club. The original lock - overlooked by the Harbour Master's classically styled house - is abandoned, but it enjoyed a brief new lease of life during the Second World War as an alternative point of entry in case of bomb damage. The lock apparatus from this period remains in place, the work of Cowans Sheldon, the Carlisle engineering firm perhaps better known for their railway cranes and turntables. A small detail, for sure, but emblematic of this resilient little port's intrinsic and abiding appeal.

Purton

Map 35

There was a tall chimnied flour mill here once, and on Derby Day they used to run their own horse race along the foreshore known as the Royal Drift. Now the chief attraction lies in the ships' graveyard and whole families are to be seen rubbing shoulders with rubbing strakes preserved, not so much in aspic, but in estuary mud.

Eating & Drinking

BERKELEY ARMS - Tel: 01453 811262. Sequestered freehouse listed on CAMRA'S National Inventory of Historic Pub Interiors. Restricted opening hours but undoubtedly well worth a pilgrimage; pubs like this are at a premium now, yet this guide boasts three!

Sharpness

Map 35

A humbler counterpart to Goole on the Yorkshire Ouse, where life revolves around the enduring relationship between tides and docks. Scintillating views down the estuary to the Severn bridges and nuclear power plants. You are reminded of the centre forward's prerequisite - a certain Sharpness in front of Goole.

Eating & Drinking

SHARPNESS DOCKERS CLUB - dock precincts. Tel: 01453 811477. You don't have to be a docker (let alone a member) to enjoy the considerable hospitality of this social club housed in what was once the Sharpness Hotel; one of three in the village. Archive scenes of the docks and railways adorn the walls, the meals are marvellous, and the beer comes from Wickwar just down the road. Oh yes, and skittles too. Perfect! GL13 9UN

PIER VIEW HOTEL - Oldminster Road. Tel: 01453 811255. Hosting the Sharpness Strongest Man Contest when we were last there. Shame we couldn't stay. GL13 9NA

Shopping

Friendly general store in dock precincts (archive postcards!). Mace convenience store and post office in village.

Connections

BUSES - Cotswold Green service 206 runs thrice to/from Dursley Mon-Sat ex Fri. 205 operates for commuters at the crack of dawn to Cam & Dursley station, returning at tea time. Tel: 0871 200 2233.

TAXIS - Castle Cars. Tel: 01453 511793.

Cotswold Canals

Stroudwater Navigation at Ebley

36 STROUDWATER NAVIGATION Framilode & Eastington 4mls/7lks

YOU need to invite two main guests to a restoration party, self-belief and money; they seldom arrive simultaneously, and even more rarely leave hand in hand. But in 1979, the late David Boakes, Secretary then to the Stroudwater Thames & Severn Canal Trust, gritted his teeth, with the determination of a non-league manager pitted against a Premiership side in the cup, and said: "We're going to win this one!" There seemed no plausible reason to doubt him.

A good deal of water has flowed under the crumbling arches of what are now collectively known as the Cotswold Canals since then. Completion dates have come and gone and the cause received a particularly vicious blow in 2008 when British Waterways, a senior partner in the project, excused themselves and left early, saying they had to spend their money somewhere else. At that point self-belief - in the shape of Stroud District Council - became the life and soul of the party and - egged-on by the Heritage Lottery Fund and other stakeholders - came up with a scheme for six miles of canal to be fully restored between Stonehouse and Brimscombe. Designated (with typically romantic institutional euphony) Phase 1a, a successful completion will see it hopefully being followed by Phase 1b, from Stonehouse to Saul and the rest of the inland waterway network.

Opened in 1779, and measuring eight miles in length with thirteen locks, the Stroudwater Navigation enjoyed considerable prosperity before the Railway Age. And even thereafter, up until the Second World War, a moderate amount of local trade, predominantly in the guise of Forest of Dean mined coal, continued to use the route.

Don't start off too quickly walking eastwards: contemplate the Severn; gaze across its broad expanse to the hilly outline of the Forest of Dean; pay a visit perhaps to St Peter's; then set your face towards the Cotswold escarpment - Sapperton Tunnel is almost twenty miles away and three hundred feet higher.

Framilode Lock was tidal and was well known to the poet and composer Ivor Gurney who kept his sailing boat *Dorothy* with the keeper. The lock lies buried in a private garden now. A reedy length of canal, more or less 'in water', runs past the Ship Inn, is culverted beneath the by-

road to Saul, then promptly peters out as the path to Saul Junction follows the southern bank of the River Frome, channelled beside pollarded willows, to reach the Gloucester & Sharpness Canal at Saul Junction.

The first few hundred yards of the Stroudwater east of Saul remained in use as linear moorings after the navigation was officially abandoned in 1954. These end abruptly at the site of Walk swing-bridge. The by-road it carried from Wheatenhurst will need to be raised to provide navigable headroom when restoration takes place.

East of here sections of the canal have been obliterated, not least an aqueduct over the River Frome. It is proposed to re-dig some of the original channel, but also to create a new line, so as to enable the canal to pass beneath the motorway where it crosses the Frome. Pending undertaking of this work as part of Phase 1b, walkers can follow at least some of the towpath as far as the site of Bristol Road Wharf before being forced into their own detour via the river bank. A fine hump-backed occupation bridge still spans this lily-rich stretch of water and two old pill-boxes permit you to indulge in fantasies of invasion and resistance.

Fromebridge Mill has been converted into a popular pub and restaurant.

Walking beside the Frome would be an idyllic exercise but for the racket emanating from the M5, an immense and unceasing barrier of noise of El Alamein artillery barrage intensity. At least, in passing through the dark confines of the tunnel beneath the motorway, you can pretend to be a rock star emerging from your dressing room to a stadium filled with roaring fans.

Passing Meadow Mill you reach the northern outskirts of the village of Eastington and rediscover the original course of the navigation at Pike Bridge, rebuilt to navigational height in 2005. Dock Lock derived its utilitarian name from the presence of the Stroudwater company's boatyard and maintenance depot at this point. Pike Lock is overlooked by a cottage which latterly provided accommodation for a lock-keeper, but which originally - and hence its name - was a toll house on the local turnpike road.

37 STROUDWATER NAVIGATION Stonehouse 4mls/6lks

BEYOND Pike Lock (Map 36) restoration has already been accomplished by the Cotswold Canals Trust as far as the Birmingham-Bristol railway. Blunder Lock is just that, having gained its amusing name from a miscalculation of water levels when the canal was being built. Newtown Lock (which commemorates David Boakes) was re-opened (in heavy rain) by the Prince of Wales in 1992. The towpath changes sides at Roving Bridge and proceeds to Bond's Mill Bridge, the world's first plastic lift bridge - sturdier than it sounds. Panoramic hill views are revealed to the south-east, down as far as Hetty Pegler's Tump.

On its high embankment, the main line railway presents an expensive challenge to the restorationists, though Network Rail are sympathetically predisposed. A culvert of navigable dimensions will have to be inserted, but the foundations of the original bridge are said to be intact. Restoration of six miles of canal between 'The Ocean' and Brimscombe (Map 38) commenced in 2006, the former being a wide lily-filled pool which probably predated construction of the canal. This pretty scene is overlooked by Stonehouse Court, an extensive Elizabethan building renovated by Lutyens and now an hotel. Next door is the charming little church of St Cyr's which apparently relinquished part of its churchyard to the canal builders. Two attractive houses abut Nutshell Bridge and are curiously linked by a passage beneath it. The route of the old Midland Railway line to Nailsworth (adopted as a cycle path) crosses the canal on a cast iron bridge and there was once a transhipment wharf here. A private swing-bridge spans the canal at Ryeford as the Cotswold Way swoops briefly down to join the canal on its hundred mile way from Chipping Campden to Bath.

Fully restored, Ryeford Locks are one of only two staircase pairs on the Cotswold Canals, the other is at Dudgrove on the Thames & Severn Canal near Lechlade. To the rear of the isolated lock cottage you can see the unusual French Gothic church tower of Bodley's hillside church at Selsley. Ebley Mill provides a handsome landmark as the navigation nears Stroud. Appropriately enough it is now the headquarters of Stroud District Council, no wonder they are enthusiastic about the lovely canal on their doorstep. The restoration of Dudbridge Locks have resulted in an ingenious hydro-electric scheme which employs excess water going down the by-washes to generate green electricity.

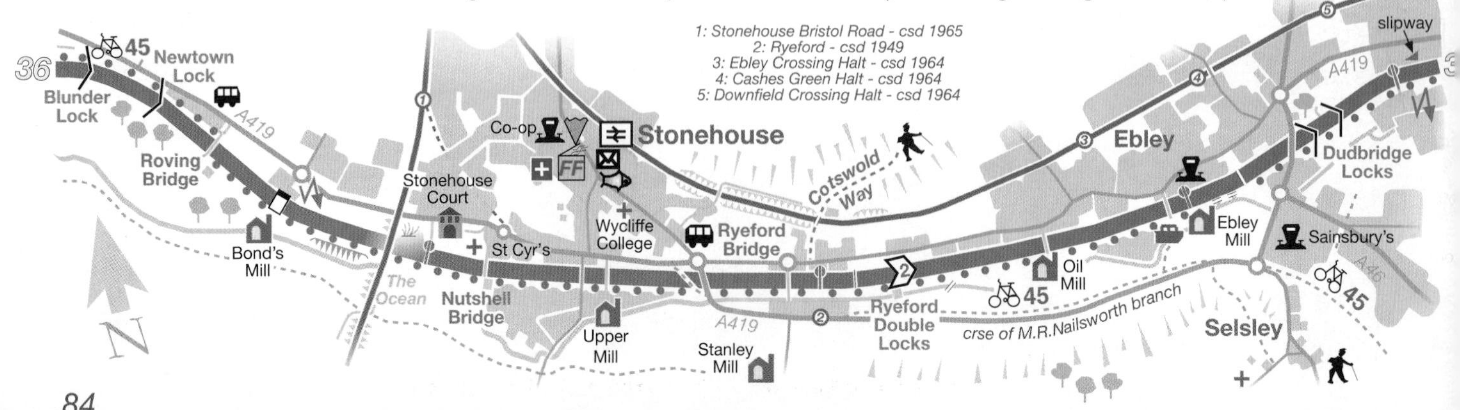

38 THAMES & SEVERN CANAL Stroud & Brimscombe 4mls/14lks

COLLECTIVELY known these days as the Cotswold Canals, the Stroudwater Navigation and Thames & Severn Canal met historically at Wallbridge Basin on the outskirts of Stroud. The latter was completed across its astonishing summit in 1789, thereby linking two of Britain's greatest rivers and providing new transport opportunities for the manufacturers of the Forest of Dean and of South Wales, not to mention the cloth-makers of the Stroud Valley. Much celebrating took place on that November day towards the end of the 18th century, and will undoubtedly do so again when, hopefully in the not too far distant future, the Severn and the Thames are reconnected.

How invigorating it must feel to live alongside this Lazarus-like canal - how satisfying to be involved in its resurrection. It must feel like perpetual Spring. By the Summer of 2016 the Stroudwater Canal was effectively navigable from 'The Ocean' (Map 37) to just short of its eastern terminus at Wallbridge. Restoration of Wallbridge Lower Lock was underway, whilst Wallbridge Upper Lock - overlooked by the Trust's excellent visitor centre - was already in working condition. The environs are fascinating, and include the site of the original Stroud Brewery, demolished in 1970.

A major challenge facing the restorationists was how to thread the Thames & Severn Canal through the railway arches at the eastern end of Stroud, the canal's original course having been obliterated by road improvements. The resulting triumph is a superbly engineered 'S' bend which will make for entertaining boating in years to come; though walkers and cyclists need to cross the road bridge and pass beneath the railway viaduct as the towpath changes sides at this point.

Bowbridge Lock was being restored by the Waterways Recovery Group on the occasion of our most recent research trip, whilst Griffin's Mill and Ham Mill locks were already fully gated. These are three of five chambers in various stages of rebirth pending Phase 1a's completion between Stroud and Brimscombe. The towpath had been upgraded through to Brimscombe, and it was heartening to see the canal gradually gaining strength, like a loved one recuperating from a long, debilitating illness. Hearing posts activate smart phone apps for interpretation of the canal's finer points, and snatches of poetry adorn wayside slates.

continued overleaf:

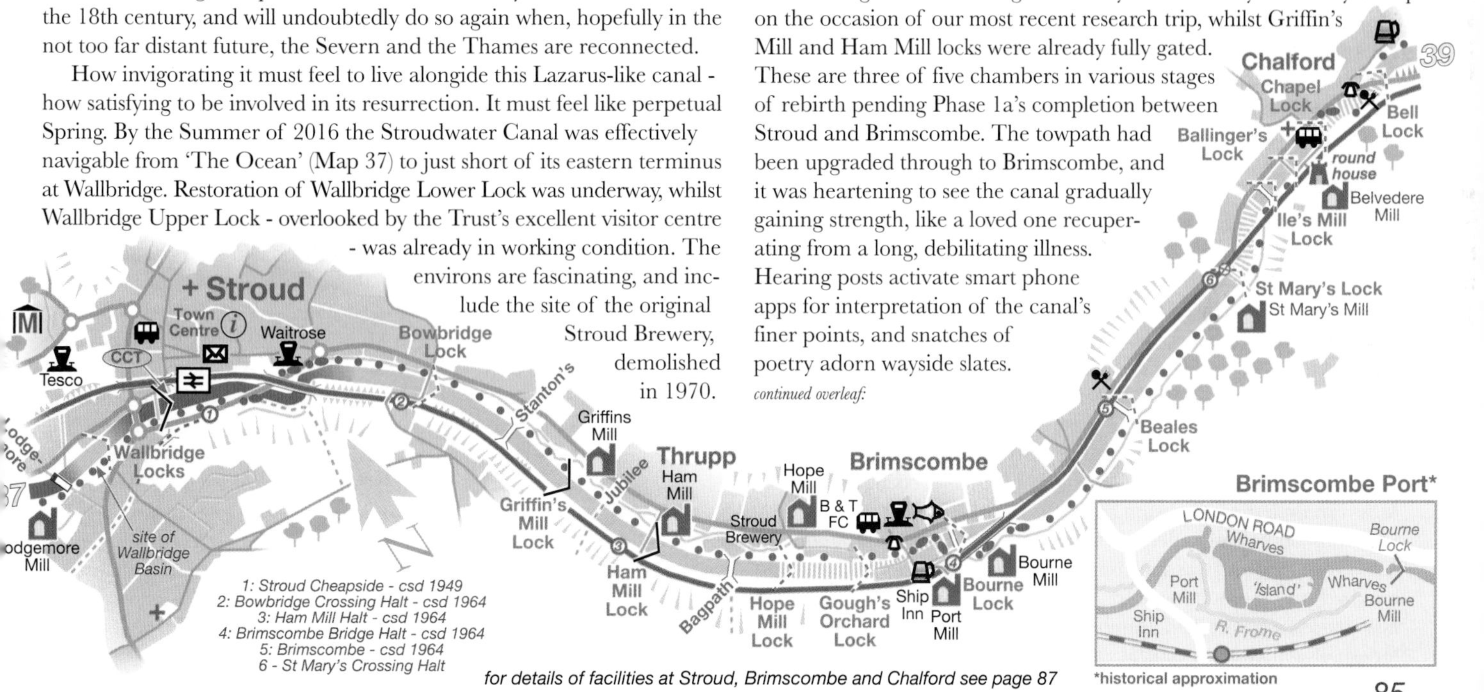

1: Stroud Cheapside - csd 1949
2: Bowbridge Crossing Halt - csd 1964
3: Ham Mill Halt - csd 1964
4: Brimscombe Bridge Halt - csd 1964
5: Brimscombe - csd 1964
6 - St Mary's Crossing Halt

for details of facilities at Stroud, Brimscombe and Chalford see page 87

*historical approximation

continued from page 85:

Most of the over-bridges are traditionally hump-backed, but Jubilee Bridge is an attractive structure of cast iron latticework, built to enable workers to reach the mills from their houses up on the hillside beyond the railway. So dense was industry in this constricted valley that the Great Western Railway opened a necklace of wayside halts served by push & pull trains whose non-stop diesel descendants continue to enliven the scene.

It is interesting to note that the last cargo of coal recorded on the Thames & Severn Canal was discharged from a barge called *Dorothy* at Ham Mill in 1933. A micro-brewery bearing the name of its illustrious predecessor has been opened in the vicinity of Hope Mill Lock, in a building known appropriately as the Phoenix Works. Present day boaters appear to have inherited the prodigious thirst of their bargee forebears and should revel in this local brew when navigation returns. Hope Mill was also the site of Abdela & Mitchell's (formerly Edwin Clarke's) boatyard, builders of river boats and pleasure steamers which saw service in some amazingly far-flung corners of the world. On the approach to Brimscombe the canal rubs shoulders with the neat little ground where Brimscombe & Thrupp Football Club play their home games in the Hellenic League.

No avid canal enthusiast would have been immune to the fascination of Brimscombe in its heyday. The need for an inland port was brought about by the necessity of transferring goods between vessels of a different gauge: Severn 'trows' and Thames barges of the 'western' kind as well as a requirement to store items pending final delivery or further transport. Locks on the Stroudwater and Thames & Severn, though widebeam, were of differing dimensions. To save water the Thames & Severn locks were reduced in length around 1841 and in the final years of trade carriers found the ubiquitous narrowboat a more suitable craft for working on the Thames & Severn than the wide-beam barges of old.

Brimscombe basin offered a hundred and seventy five thousand square feet of capacity and was said to have been able to accommodate up to a hundred vessels simultaneously. Notable features included the company's head offices, a transit shed, warehousing and a boat weighing machine used for establishing tolls. A central island was incorporated for the secure storage of goods which might, unprotected, have caught the attention of the thieving classes. The main warehouse found unusual use as a school following the demise of the canal and was unfortunately demolished in 1964. The most handsome survival is Port Mill, premises now of the History Press, whose list appropriately contains many titles devoted to the history of canals. Proposals for the commerical redevelopment of the port are understandably in a state of flux, but it will play a vital role in funding the restoration. At present one of the largest premises serves as an indoor football facility. Walkers face a short detour (follow the Thames & Severn Way arrows) before regaining the line of the canal by Bourne Lock, beyond which the canal is punctured again by the railway, thereafter re-establishing itself as far as Chalford, a beguiling section upon which the Golden Valley casts its not inconsiderable spell.

Brimscombe railway station boasted a small engine shed for stabling bankers for the climb to Sapperton summit. On to St Mary's, canal and railway - accompanied by the Frome chuckling transparently over it's clear gravel bed - create a mutually exclusive environment away from the traffic on the A419. An access lane to St Mary's Mill swoops down to cross the railway by way of a traditionally-gated level crossing guarded by a tiny signal box. Piped beneath the railway yet again, the canal briefly loses confidence before reappearing at Ile's Lock overlooked by a mellow and now domesticised Clayfield Mill.

It grows increasingly difficult not to be overawed by the beauty of the canal's surroundings, as indeed was Temple Thurston on his famous voyage along the canal with the *Flower of Gloster* in 1910. He likened the surrounding scenery to Switzerland, something hacks are over-inclined to do when faced with precipitously hilly districts of England. Nevertheless his heart was in the right place and you too will be entranced by these 'blue slate roofs' viewed against a 'golden distance'. At Chalford you come upon the first of the Thames & Severn's keynote roundhouses and a gable end advertising 'James Smart - Coal, Stone & Sand Merchant, Dealer in Staffordshire Bricks'. Smart's barges traded here until the canal was formally abandoned.

Stonehouse Map 37

Stonehouse will come into its own when boaters begin to use the Stroudwater Navigation once again. In the meantime, walkers will probably want to press on to Stroud where the facilities are closer to hand. Wycliffe College was founded in 1882. The remains of its original boathouse still stand beside the canal, though nowadays the boat crews are put through their paces on the Gloucester & Sharpness Canal at Saul Junction.

Stroud Map 38

A codicil to the Cotswolds, with a spirited tradition of independent outlook, the textile town of Stroud tumbles down the valley side with the profile of a dry ski slope. Gradients apart, Stroud is a likeable place to wander around, several fine buildings vying for attention, none finer than the splendidly classical Subscription Rooms of 1833. In its heyday as a wool town Stroud was famous for its military tunics, now those mills left in production - out of the hundred and fifty which once functioned in the Frome Valley - are renowned for snooker table cloth and Wimbledon tennis ball felt.

Eating & Drinking

UPPER LOCK CAFE - Wallbridge. Tel: 01453 297172. Amiable refreshment stop handily placed beside Wallbridge Upper Lock and the CCT visitor centre. Nice old T&S map on the wall. GL5 3JS

WOODRUFFS ORGANIC CAFE - High Street. Tel: 01453 759195. Exemplifies Stroud in both outlook and atmosphere; heavenly cakes. GL5 1AJ

DINNER AT SIX - Union Street. Tel: 01453 758477. Stylish cafe/restaurant open Tue-Sat 10am-3pm and 6pm-11pm. GL5 2HE

Shopping

Stroud's precipitous High Street is refreshingly bereft of chain stores (they lurk down in the ubiquitous Merrywalks Shopping Centre and can, as such, be left to their own anodyne devices) and congenially populated by individual retailers of more enterprising outlook, notably Inprint, a stylish secondhand bookshop with a choice collection of local subject matter. A few doors downhill lies Stroud Bookshop, an increasingly rare example of an independently owned new bookdealer. Made in Stroud on Kendrick Street reflects the area's status as a haven for craftsmen and artists.

Things to Do

TOURIST INFORMATION - Subscription Rooms, George Street. Tel: 01453 760960. GL5 1AE

THE MUSEUM IN THE PARK - Stratford Park. Tel: 01453 763394. Local heritage. GL5 4AF

Connections

TRAINS - hourly Great Western Railway services along the Golden Valley to/from Gloucester (via Stonehouse) and Swindon with bi-hourly through trains to/from London Paddington. Tel: 03457 484950.

BUSES - Stagecoach/Cotswold Green services throughout the area. Service 54/54A threads its way approximately bi-hourly through the Golden Valley via Brimscombe, Chalford and Sapperton to Cirencester Mon-Sat and is consequently of good use to Thames & Severn towpath walkers. Tel: 0871 200 2233.

TAXIS - A&A. Tel: 01453 767777.

Brimscombe Map 38

The world's first lawn mower was made at the Phoenix Works, now home to the Stroud Brewery, whose wares you can sample on tap. Facilities for passing walkers include fish & chips and a convenience store.

Eating & Drinking

SHIP INN - Tel: 01453 884388. Pub with Severn Trow on its sign. Open lunch & evening daily. GL5 2QN

Chalford Map 39

Cuddled in the lap of the Golden Valley, Chalford deserves to be savoured in its own right rather than just an adjunct to the canal. Indeed, there is something to be said for the walker detouring along the gorgeous by-road between Bell Lock and Valley Lock to get a more intimate view of the higgledy-piggledy houses which define its character. Railway enthusiasts will remember Chalford as the eastern terminus of a push & pull service from Gloucester until 1964.

LAVENDER BAKEHOUSE - London Road. Tel: 01453 889239. Superb cafe serving breakfasts (from 9am) lunches and teas. Upstairs gallery. GL6 8NW

Connections

BUSES - Cotswold Green service 54/A runs Mon-Sat between Stroud and Cirencester calling also at Sapperton. Tel: 0871 200 2233.

Sapperton Map 39

Idyllic settlement perched above its famous tunnel offering easy access to view the western portal. Historic links with proponents of the Arts & Crafts movement.

Eating & Drinking

DANEWAY INN - Tel: 01285 760297. Characterful 'canalside' inn known as the Bricklayers Arms when the Thames & Severn was open. Re-opened after refurbishment 2016. A spot of food and a pint of Wadworth will set you up for the walk over the top of Sapperton Tunnel. GL7 6AN

Kemble Map 40

Tudoresque railhead ideal for exploring the eastern end of Sapperton Tunnel and the source of the Thames.

Eating & Drinking

TUNNEL HOUSE INN - Tel: 01285 770280. Picturesque pub adjacent eastern portal of Sapperton Tunnel and open from 11am daily. GL7 6PW

Connections

TRAINS - as Stroud.

39 THAMES & SEVERN CANAL Chalford & Daneway 5mls/14lks

PENNINE overtones assail the Thames & Severn as it climbs through the Golden Valley. The Cotswold landscape is softer of course, yet you are still reminded of the constricted valleys of the Calder or the Colne, the Tame or the Roch. Here it was the course of the Frome which aided and abetted the canal builders, and the little river comes flowing transparently down its valley with the self-confidence of a child empowered by an important errand.

Thicker and thicker grow the locks, and the walker feels the climb, though not as much as the boaters will once navigation is restored. Clowes Bridge gained its name from the canal's resident engineer, Josiah, the man responsible for realising Robert Whitworth's blueprints in bricks and mortar. Narrowing, the constricted valley suffers lack of space, its hillside houses, so mellow, so apparently organic in origin, scattered haphazardly on shelves and terraces like the contents of a corner shop.

With the railway - engineered by Isambard Kingdom Brunel, and opened to the Broad Gauge in 1845 - intent on climbing harder, faster and attached to the neighbouring ridge on a remarkable sequence of blue brick viaducts (originally of typically Brunellian timber construction) the canal reaches Valley Lock, whereafter the houses and mills are largely left behind and woodland creates a very real sense of remoteness. In these very woods, while Eynsham Harry prepared a mid-day meal of wild hops, Temple Thurston counted seventeen varieties of wild flower. Short-changed by poetic impulse, Pearson was much more attracted to the redbrick and rounded windows of Chalford's erstwhile waterworks. Dating from 1890, quite late in the canal's commercial career, coal for the furnaces was brought in by boat. On the towpath a milepost informs you that you have journeyed five miles from Wallbridge (Stroud) and that a further twenty-three and three-quarters remain to be covered before reaching the Thames at Inglesham.

By Baker's Mill Upper Lock the Frome widens into a reservoir created by the canal company for water supplies. In doing so they were forced to acquire Puck's Mill in 1791 and close it down in order to guarantee a sufficient head of water.

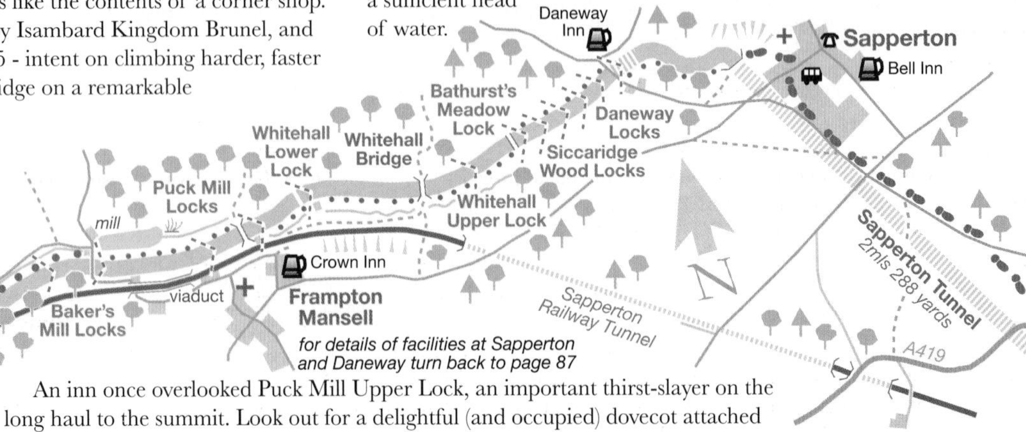

for details of facilities at Sapperton and Daneway turn back to page 87

An inn once overlooked Puck Mill Upper Lock, an important thirst-slayer on the long haul to the summit. Look out for a delightful (and occupied) dovecot attached to the end wall of a canalside house above the lock: footpaths splay off into the woods, agitating to be explored.

The Golden Valley lives up to the implications of its name as the canal winds through woodland never out of earshot of the Frome. Walkers on the Thames & Severn towpath are joined by fellow travellers on the Wysis

Way, a 55 mile path linking Offa's Dyke with the Thames Path. 'WD 1784' engraved on the arch of Whitehall Bridge refers to the mason William Dennis responsible for constructing this section of the canal. You are now entering the Sapperton Valley Reserve of the Gloucestershire Wildlife Trust.

Even in the canal's heyday, working up or down the final flight of seven locks to and from the summit at Daneway was often problematical given the paucity of water supply. Consumption was reduced by about 20% following shortening of the lock chambers. A series of sideponds had already been added in 1823, but every drop of water continued to count. By 1893 matters had grown so bad that the canal east of Chalford was closed. It re-opened six years later, but was still wracked by water problems. Encountering just one other boat (captained by an elderly lady humming quietly to herself at the tiller) Temple Thurston remarked that in places they barely floated at all, much to the chagrin of Fanny the boat horse. A quarter of a century later the author Geoffrey Boumphrey and a companion were unable to progress this far even by canoe as described in his book *Down River*, an account of a tour on the Severn and the Thames and, where possible, the Cotswold Canals, published in 1936. In the event Boumphrey and his pal 'George' had to portage their canoes by car between Chalford and Cricklade. They must have been reading William Bliss's, *Art and Practise of Canoeing on English Rivers, Navigations and Canals*, which records that he was charged 25 shillings to have his own canoe conveyed by road between Chalford and Cricklade.

The canal widened into a wharf and basin between the two Daneway locks, the upper of which was overlooked by an inn, once the Bricklayer's Arms now The Daneway Inn. The higher lock has been infilled to provide the pub with a car park; future patrons of the beer garden will have the preferable ring-side view of an excavated lock chamber.

The summit lies 362 feet above sea level, but it rapidly becomes apparent as you twist in an easterly, becoming south-easterly direction away from Daneway, that the canal can go no further save by subterranean methods. And indeed, within less than half a mile, the neighbouring ridge rears suddenly up in defiance and the western portal of Sapperton is revealed, battlemented as if it means business; an entrance into Hades embowered by wild garlic.

3,808 yards long (impressive enough, but roundly beaten by the Huddersfield Narrow Canal's Standedge tunnel which is 5,698 yards long) and up to 200 feet below the surface of the Cotswold landscape it burrows through, Sapperton Tunnel was five years in the making. George III came to inspect it on Saturday 19th July 1788 as an antidote to taking the waters in nearby Cheltenham. Contemporary accounts suggest that His Majesty expressed astonishment. So, more practically, did Temple Thurston, who lay on his back with Eynsham Harry for four damp and sepulchral hours to propel the *Flower of Gloster* through the tunnel in time honoured fashion. Curiously, he refers to a barge in a lock and the dazzling light of the setting sun when he emerges from the tunnel's eastern portal. Disorientation, or poetic licence? In its working days a four-hourly cycle of entry times was the order of the day. A realisitic account of a boat being legged through the tunnel enlivens the opening pages of C. S. Forester's adventure *Hornblower and the Atropos*. Pending restoration, we have to walk across the top in the footsteps of the old boat horses and mules. For a heady moment one imagines that the dung on the road through Sapperton village is still steaming from those animals, until it becomes apparent that horse-riding is a popular activity amongst the rides of Oakley Wood.

40 THAMES & SEVERN CANAL Coates & Kemble 4mls/0lks

WALKING over the top of Sapperton tunnel gives you plenty of time to marvel at its existence ... and perhaps yours as well. From time to time you catch sight of spoil heaps planted with beech trees which bring to mind all the activity of those human moles who dug the tunnel over two centuries ago. Spare a thought too for the almost parallel railway tunnel completed in 1845, a mere 1 mile and 95 yards in length. This is said to have been bored outwards from vertical shafts because the railway company wasn't yet in possession of the land at either end!

If you were enamoured of the Gothic portal at the western end of the canal tunnel, you will be surprised to discover, not a mirror image at the eastern end, but a design of quite different Classical style: a sort of double A-side in pop single terms. Above, and to the left of the portal, stands the Tunnel House Inn, erected during construction of the canal to provide accommodation and refreshment. It still fulfils the latter purpose admirably, though the original third storey was destroyed by fire in 1952. The inn was once visited by John Betjeman and his father.

Coates Roundhouse differs from Chalford in that its conical roof is inverted as a means of gathering water for domestic use. Forcibly closed on health grounds in the 1950s, it now resembles an abandoned lighthouse.

The summit section of the Thames & Severn is 8 miles and 13 chains in length. Sadly the canal east of Sapperton is not so well-defined as in the Golden Valley, and at Coatesfield Bridge it ceases to be a right of way. Long distance walkers are not, however, abandoned to their own devices for too long, a couple of fields away lies the official source of the River Thames and the commencement of the Thames Path, London being a mere 184 miles away.

The old course of the canal encounters an even older transport link, the Roman's Fosse Way, and comes upon the site of a pumping house which supplied three million gallons of much-needed water a day to the summit. And there, alas, we must jump ship, halfway between Stroud and Lechlade. Kemble's lovely railway station lies close at hand and forms a fitting sort of ending in its own right.

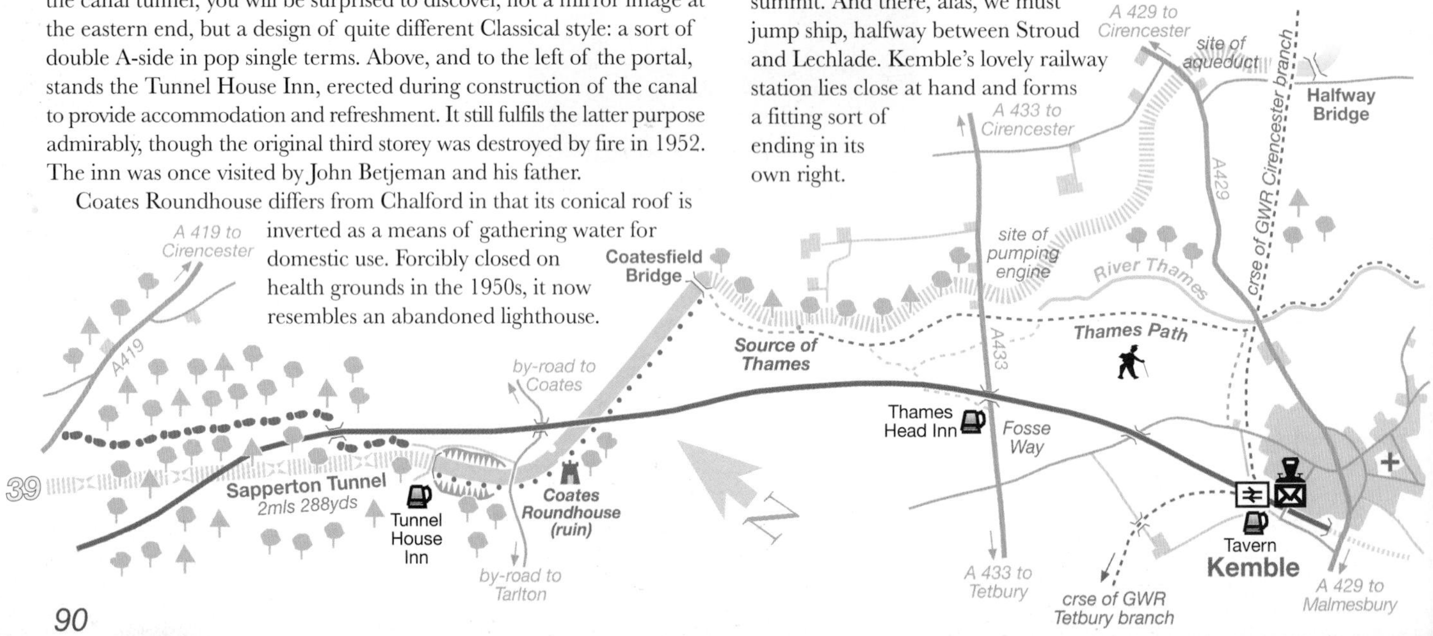

Sapperton West

Sapperton East

Coates Roundhouse

This Guide

Pearson's Canal Companions are a long established, independently produced series of guide books devoted to the inland waterways and designed to appeal equally to boaters, walkers, cyclists and other, less readily pigeon-holed members of society. Considerable pride is taken to make these guides as up to date, accurate, entertaining and inspirational as possible. A good guide book should fulfil three functions: make you want to go; interpret the lie of the land when you're there; and provide a lasting souvenir of your journeys.

The Maps

There are forty numbered maps whose layout is shown by the Route Planner inside the front cover. Maps 1 to 7 cover the River Avon upstream from Tewkesbury; Maps 8 to 13 cover the Stratford Canal from Stratford to King's Norton; Maps 14 to 20 the Worcester & Birmingham Canal between Birmingham and Worcester; Maps 21 & 22 the newly opened Droitwich Canals; Maps 23 to 31 the River Severn downstream from Stourport to Gloucester; Maps 32 to 35 the Gloucester & Sharpness Canal; and Maps 36 to 40 the as yet largely unnavigable Cotswold Canals from Saul Junction to the summit beyond Sapperton tunnel.

The maps - measured imperially like the waterways they depict, and not being slavishly north-facing - are easily read in either direction. Users will thus find most itineraries progressing smoothly and logically from left to right or vice versa. Figures quoted at the top of each map refer to distance per map, locks per map and average cruising time. An alternative indication of timings from centre to centre can be found on the Route Planner. Obviously, cruising times vary with the nature of your boat and the number of crew at your disposal, so quoted times should be taken only as an estimate. Neither do times quoted take into account any delays which might occur at lock flights in high season. Walking and cycling times will depend

INFORMATION

very much on the state of individual sections of towpath and the stamina of those concerned.

The Text

Each map is accompanied by a route commentary placing the waterway in its historic, social and topographical context. As close to each map as is feasible, gazetteer-like entries are given for places passed through, listing, where appropriate, facilities of significance to users of this guide. Every effort is made to ensure these details are as up to date as possible, but - especially where pubs/restaurants are concerned - we suggest you telephone ahead if relying upon an entry to provide you with a meal at any given time.

Walking

The simplest way to go canal exploring is on foot along the towpaths originally provided so that horses could 'tow' boats. Walking costs little more than the price of shoe leather and you are free to concentrate on the passing scene; something that boaters, with the responsibilities of navigation thrust upon them, are not always at liberty to do. The maps set out to give some idea of the quality of the towpath on any given section of canal. More of an art than a science to be sure, but at least it reflects our personal experiences, and whilst it does vary from area to area, none of it should prove problematical for anyone inured to the vicissitudes of country walking.

We recommend the use of public transport to facilitate 'one-way' itineraries but stress the advisability of checking up to date details on the telephone numbers quoted, or on the websites of National Rail Enquiries or Traveline for trains and buses respectively.

Walking beside rivers is not always so easy. Over the centuries landowners have appropriated many ancient rights of way, whilst the demise of former ferries has also broken links which once existed. Fortunately, the Avon and the Severn are both accompanied by waymarked long distance paths - Shakespeare's Avon Way and the Severn Way respectively - and both routes are shown on the accompanying maps, though the additional use of an up to date Ordnance Survey Landranger or Explorer sheet is recommended. Should you be considering walking the full length of these paths over several consecutive days, Tourist Information Centres can usually be relied upon to offer accommodation advice.

Cycling

Bicycling along towpaths is an increasingly popular pastime, though one not always equally popular with other waterway users such as boaters, anglers and pedestrians. It is important to remember that you are sharing the towpath with other people out for their own form of enjoyment, and to treat them with the respect and politeness they deserve. A bell is a useful form of diplomacy; failing that, a stentorian cough, or the ability to whistle tuneful extracts from popular operas. Happily, since the Canal & River Trust took over from British Waterways, it is no longer necessary to carry a permit to cycle along the towpath.

Boating

Boating on inland waterways is an established, though relatively small, facet of the UK tourist industry. It is also, increasingly, a chosen lifestyle. There are approximately 30,000 privately owned boats registered on the canals, but in addition to these, numerous firms offer boats for hire. These range from small operators with half a dozen boats to sizeable fleets run by companies with several bases.

Most hire craft have all the creature comforts you are likely to expect. In the excitement of planning a boating holiday you may give scant thought to the contents of your hire boat, but at the end of a hard day's boating such matters take on more significance, and a well equipped, comfortable boat, large enough to accommodate your crew with something to spare, can make the difference between a good holiday and one which will be shudderingly remembered for the wrong reasons.

Traditionally, hire boats are booked out by the week or fortnight, though many firms now offer more flexible short breaks or extended weeks. All reputable hire firms give newcomers tuition in boat handling and lock working, and first-timers soon find themselves adapting to the pace of things 'on the cut'.

H & G milepost, Over

Navigational Advice

Newcomers, hiring a boat on the inland waterways for the first time, have every right to expect sympathetic and thorough tuition from the company providing their boat. Boat-owners are, by definition, likely to be already adept at navigating. The following, however, may prove useful points of reference.

Locks are part of the charm of canal cruising, but they are potentially dangerous environments for children, pets and careless adults. Use of them should be methodical and unhurried, whilst special care should be exercised in rain, frost and snow when slippery hazards abound.

The locks included in this guide fall into two distinct types: narrow and wide. The narrow locks are to be found on the Stratford, Worcester & Birmingham and Droitwich Junction canals. The wide locks are on the River Avon and Droitwich Barge Canal. These locks can usually accept narrowbeam craft side by side and it helps save water (not to mention work-load) if they are shared with other boats travelling in the same direction. The locks on the River Severn are large, mechanically-operated and under the control of keepers. Boaters joining the Severn at Stourport, Hawford and Worcester are recommended to telephone ahead to the first lock they will encounter to let the keeper know they're coming.

Finally, it behoves us all to be on our best behaviour at locks. Remember to exercise a little 'give and take'. The use of foul mouths or fists to decide precedence at locks is one canal tradition not worthy of preservation.

Mooring on the canals featured in this guide is per usual practice - ie on the towpath side, away from sharp bends, bridge-holes and narrows. A 'yellow' bollard symbol represents visitor mooring sites; either as designated officially or, in some cases as recommended by our personal experience. Of course, one of the great joys of canal boating has always been the ability to moor wherever (sensibly) you like. In recent years, however, it has become obvious, particularly in urban areas, that there are an increasing number of undesirable locations where mooring is not to be recommended for fear of vandalism, theft or abuse. It would be nice if local authorities would see their way to providing pleasant, secure, overnight facilities for passing boaters who, after all, bring the commerce of tourism in their wake. Few boaters would object to making a small payment in such circumstances, as is the custom on a number of river navigations.

continued overleaf:

continued from page 93:

River moorings are not as easily come by as those on canals, mostly because the banks are in private ownership. On the Avon and the Severn, therefore, it's wise to plan ahead and identify in advance where you plan to moor for a lunchtime stop or overnight. In addition to the visitor mooring symbols depicted on the maps, many riverside inns also offer mooring facilities for patrons. At busy times designated moorings can quickly fill-up and mooring alongside other boats (with co-operation, obviously) may provide a solution.

Turning points on the canals are known as 'winding holes'; pronounced as the thing which blows because in the old days the wind was expected to do much of the work rather than the boatman. Winding holes capable of taking a full length boat of around seventy foot length are marked where appropriate on the maps. Winding holes capable of turning shorter craft are marked with the approximate length. It is of course possible to turn boats at junctions and at most boatyards, though in the case of the latter it is considered polite to seek permission before doing so.

Boating facilities are provided at regular intervals along the inland waterways, and range from a simple water tap or refuse disposal skip, to the provision of sewage disposal, showers and laundry. Such vital features are also obtainable at boatyards and marinas along with repairs and servicing. An alphabetical list of boatyards appears opposite.

Closures (or 'stoppages' in canal parlance) traditionally occur on the inland waterways between November and April, when most of the heavy maintenance work is undertaken. Occasionally, however, an emergency stoppage, or perhaps water restriction, may be imposed at short notice, closing part of the route you intend to use. Up to date details are available on *www.canalrivertrust.org.uk* or from hire bases.

Chalford

Canal & River Trust

The Canal & River Trust oversee all the canals and river navigations contained within this guide with the exception of the River Avon. Their Head Office is located at: First Floor North, Station House, 500 Elder Gate, Milton Keynes MK9 1BB *www.canalrivertrust.org.uk* Members of the public can make enquiries at CART's Customer Service Centre at Cambrian Wharf in Birmingham 10am-2pm Mons and 11am-2pm Weds & Fris; and at Gloucester Waterways Museum daily between 11am and 3pm. Otherwise, the best means of making contact is via the internet or by telephoning: 0303 040 4040.

Avon Navigation Trust

This body oversees the upkeep and maintenance of the River Avon between Tewkesbury and Stratford. Their headquarters are at: Mill Wharf, Wyre Piddle, Pershore, Worcs WR10 2JF. Tel: 01386 552517.

ANT offer an extremely useful 'River Watch' scheme linked to a series of live web cams which provide 'real time' details of water levels, mooring occupancies and weather reports. *www.avonnavigationtrust.org*

Cotswold Canals Trust

The Cotswold Canals Trust have visitor centres at Saul (GL2 7LA - Tel: 0785 402 6504) and Stroud (GL5 3JS - Tel: 0758 228 6636). They operate boat trips and charters at Saul and Ebley - Tel: 0796 082 1642.

Societies

The Inland Waterways Association was founded in 1946 to campaign for the retention of the canal system. Many routes now open to pleasure boaters may not have been so but for this organisation. Membership details, together with details of the IWA's regional branches, may be obtained from: Inland Waterways Association, Island House, Moor Road, Chesham HP5 1WA. Tel: 01494 783453. *www.waterways.org.uk* A number of the canals featured in this guide are also supported by individual groups who will advertise their presence locally or on the internet.

Acknowledgements

Grateful thanks: to Meg Gregory for the sign-written cover artwork; to the late Robin Smithett for additional photography; to Andy Berry of the Cotswold Canals Trust; to Clive Matthews of the Avon Navigation Trust; to Karen Tanguy who facilitated the author's research trips and generally ensured the book's smooth passage to the printers; and to those selfsame printers, Hawksworth of Uttoxeter, and all their splendid staff.

BOATING DIRECTORY

Hire Bases

ABC BOAT HIRE - Alvechurch, Worcester & Birmingham Canal, Map 16; Worcester, Worcester & Birmingham Canal, Map 20. PO Box 232 Worcester WR1 2SD Tel: 0330 3330 590 *www.abcboathire.com*

ANGLO WELSH WATERWAY HOLIDAYS - Wootton Wawen, Stratford-on-Avon Canal, Map 9; Tardebigge, Worcs & Birmingham Canal, Map 17 . 2 The Hide Market, West Street, Bristol BS2 0BH. Tel: 0117 304 1122 *www.anglowelsh.co.uk*

BLACK PRINCE HOLIDAYS - Stoke Wharf, Worcester & Birmingham Canal, Map 17. Stoke Prior, Bromsgrove, Worcestershire B60 4LA. Tel: 01527 575115 *www.black-prince.com*

BROOK LINE - Oddingley, Worcester & Birmingham Canal, Map 19. Dunhampstead Wharf, Oddingley, Droitwich, Worcs. WR9 7JX Tel: 01905 773889. *www.brook-line.co.uk*

EXCELLENCE AFLOAT - Stratford-on-Avon, Stratford Canal, Map 8. Western Road, Stratford-on-Avon, Warks CV37 0AH. Tel: 0247 639 3333. *www.valleycruises.co.uk*

STARLINE - Staffs & Worcs Canal, Map 23. Engine Lane, Stourport, Worcs DY13 9EP. Tel: 01531 632003. *www.starlinenarrowboats.co.uk*

Boatyards

ANGLO WELSH - Wootton Wawen, Stratford Canal, Map 9. Tel: 01564 793427. B95 6BZ

ANGLO WELSH - Tardebigge, Worcester & Birmingham Canal, Map 17. Tel: 01527 873898. B60 1LR

ALVECHURCH MARINA - Alvechurch, Worcester & Birmingham Canal, Map 16. Tel: 0121 445 1133. B48 7SQ

BIDFORD BOATS - Bidford, River Avon, Map 6. Tel: 01789 772124. B50 4JJ

BLACK PRINCE Stoke Wharf, Worcester & Birmingham Canal. Map 17. Tel: 01527 575115. B60 4LA

BREDON MARINA - Bredon, River Avon, Map 1. Tel: 01684 773166. GL20 3XZ

BROOK LINE - Oddingley, Worcester & Birmingham Canal, Map 19. Tel: 01905 773889. WR9 7JX

R.W. DAVIS & SON - Saul, Gloucester & Sharpness Canal, Map 33. Tel: 01452 740233. GL2 7LA

DIGLIS MARINA - Worcester & Birmingham Canal, Map 20. Tel: 01905 356314. WR5 3BW

DROITWICH SPA MARINA - Droitwich Canal, Maps 18 & 22. Tel: 07970 626807. WR9 7DU

EVESHAM MARINA - Evesham, River Avon, Map 4. Tel: 01386 768500. WR11 3XZ

LIMEKILN CHANDLERS - Stourport, Staffs & Worcs Canal, Map23. Tel: 01299 821111. DY13 9EL

FRANK LYONS - Warstock, Stratford-on-Avon Canal, Map 13. Tel: 0121 474 4977. B14 4SP

JOHN PINDER & SONS - Worcester & B'ham Canal, Stoke Prior, Map 17. Tel: 01527 876438. B60 4JZ

SANKEY MARINE - Evesham, River Avon, Map 4. Tel: 01386 442338. WR11 4TA

SAUL JUNCTION MARINA - Saul, Gloucester & Sharpness Canal, Map 33. Tel: 01452 740941. GL2 7JY

SHARPNESS MARINE - Sharpness, Gloucester & Sharpness, Map 35. Tel: 01453 811476. GL13 9UN

STRENSHAM MILL - Strensham, River Avon, Map 2. Tel: 01684 274244. WR8 9LB

SWALLOW CRUISERS - Hockley Heath, Stratford Canal, Map 11. Tel: 01564 783442. B94 5NR

TEWKESBURY MARINA - Tewkesbury, River Avon, Map 1. Tel: 01684 293737. GL20 5BY

UPTON MARINA - Upton-on-Severn, River Severn, Map 28. Tel: 01684 594287. WR8 0PB

VALLEY BOAT SERVICES - Stratford-on-Avon, Stratford Canal, Map 8. Tel: 02476 393 333. CV37 0AH

WARINGS GREEN WHARF - Illshaw Heath, Stratford Canal, Map 12. Tel: 0787 981 8456. B94 6BU

WELFORD BOAT STATION - Welford, River Avon, Map 6. Tel: 01789 750878. CV37 8PP

WORCESTER MARINA - Lowesmoor Wharf, Worcester, Map 20. Tel: 01905 734160. WR1 2RS

WYRE BOATYARD - Wyre Piddle, River Avon. Map 3. Tel: 01386 860063. WR10 2JF

Day Boat Hire

ANGLO WELSH - Wootton Wawen, Stratford Canal, Map 9. Tel: 01564 793427, Worcester & Birmingham Canal, Map 17. Tel: 01527 873898.

AVON BOATING - Stratford-on-Avon, River Avon, Map 7. Motor and rowing boats. Tel: 01789 267073.

BIDFORD BOATS - Bidford, River Avon, Map 6. Tel: 01789 772124.

GLOUCESTER NARROWBOATS - Gloucester, Gloucester & Sharpness Canal, Map 31. Tel: 0777 446 4555.

HANDSAM - Evesham, River Avon, Map 4. Motor and rowing boats. Tel: 0786 089 5416.

PITCHCROFT - Worcester, River Severn, Map 25. Motor and rowing boats. Tel: 01905 27949.

Nine More Reasons for Exploring the Canals with Pearsons

9th edition - ISBN 978 0 9562777 4 9

10th edition - ISBN 978 0 9562777 8 7

10th edition - ISBN 978 0 9928492 2 1

1st edition - ISBN 978 0 9928492 1 4

8th edition - ISBN 978 0 9562777 2 5

9th edition - ISBN 978 0 9562777 3 2

8th edition - ISBN 978 0 9562777 9 4

1st edition - ISBN 978 0 9928492 0 7

3rd edition - ISBN 978 0 9562777 6 3

Pearson's Canal Companions are published by Wayzgoose. They are widely available from hire bases, boatyards, canal shops, good bookshops, via Amazon and other internet outlets.